The Age of Television:
Experiences and Theories

Milly Buonanno

Translated by Jennifer Radice

To Giovanni, the writer, with love

The Age of Television: Experiences and Theories

Milly Buonanno

Translated by Jennifer Radice

intellect Bristol, UK / Chicago, USA

First Published in the UK in 2008 by
Intellect Books, PO Box 862, Bristol BS99 1DE, UK

First published in the USA in 2007 by
Intellect Books, The University of Chicago Press, 1427 E. 60th Street, Chicago,
IL 60637, USA

A catalogue record for this book is available from the British Library.

Cover Design: Gabriel Solomons
Copy Editor: Holly Spradling
Typesetting: Mac Style, Nafferton, E. Yorkshire

ISBN 978-1-84150-181-9

Printed and bound by Gutenberg Press, Malta

CONTENTS

FOREWORD

Horace Newcomb

In the second chapter of this elegant exploration of television Milly Buonanno provides a key indication of the overall direction of her investigation.

> ...it is precisely because television allows us to switch between looking and listening, between involvement and detachment, and because it offers us both demanding and relaxing forms of cultural entertainment and social participation, that it can claim to possess the true and authentically distinctive qualities of an open medium. It is flexible; and it is resistant both to theoretical imposition and to the empirical experience of fixed, innate and unchanging characteristics (p. 41).

What a refined description, what a provocative image – the figure of flexible resistance to both theory and experience – emerges in this last sentence. 'Slippery' could be another term, and it could describe well the encounters experienced by anyone who has attempted to study television in any comprehensive manner. How, how in the world, can any 'theoretical imposition' capture the rowdy complexity of television? Put another way, why would there be any compulsion to 'fully' explain it, to suggest that our experience of it could be defined or described as 'fixed, innate and unchanging?' Yet, as Buonanno knows well, such attempts have been repeatedly made. Some have attempted to wrap theory around the entire enterprise of television while others have 'merely' tried to 'determine' key features. Gracefully, then, and with great scholarly generosity toward work that has gone before, she leads us through the terrain of television, as experienced and theorized, forgotten, recalled, and anticipated, always with its flexibility immediately before us.

In covering this ground the book becomes a map. For a while the surroundings seem familiar. Then Buonanno begins to explore from different perspectives, changing vantage points. We begin to see new angles. The shifting angles allow light to fall in different directions. Old corners are illuminated, colours are changed, shadows altered. The subtlety of these steps requires of us a kind of modesty in our movements, a sense that what may lie ahead is already prepared by the turns we have just taken.

A central aspect in the process is Buonanno's appropriate insistence that a key to finding our way is the 'connectedness' linking television to other communicative forms and to other varieties of experience.

Compared to previous 'ages', the age of mass communications is the shortest so far. It dates from the first decades of the nineteenth century and has thus lasted barely two centuries; yet in that time we have seen four major means of communication come successively into being: the press, the cinema, radio and television. The fact that all four modern forms of mass communication are present and well established in the world of today, alongside more traditional forms of communication (as well as the newest arrivals, the computer and the Internet) clearly demonstrates that these different forms are not substitutes for, but additions to, each other: they co-exist. This cumulative rather than substitutive quality of the course taken by the history of communication is the fundamental lesson imparted by the transitions theory. I am compelled to acknowledge at this point that what I define later on as the 'connective approach' is in large measure a tribute to this lesson, and more generally to a cognitive style that prefers to take co-existence and combinations into consideration (the form 'both...and' or the inclusive distinction) in preference to substitutions or dichotomies (the form 'either...or', or the exclusive distinction); (both definitions are taken from Ulrich Beck, 2003, pp. 12–15.). (p. 12)

Crucial to the great utility of the map that follows from this beginning is the recognition that this 'connectedness', this 'both...and' approach applies not only to television itself and the layers of history accumulated in its configurations, but also to the theories that attempt general explanations, the analyses of specific qualities, the histories of technologies and policies, and the critical examinations of its range of content. Buonanno's own chart of television, then, is "both" a critical exploration of the approaches of others "and" a new diagram of previous work. Here, too, as with the medium itself, she is comfortable critiquing major previous efforts and at the same time, fully at ease in acknowledging appropriating useful guidelines and cleared paths. She knows that a successful entry into the flexibly resistant jungle of television and television studies requires every useful marker at hand, especially if the ultimate goal is a major new synthesis, as is the case here.

For example, in tracing the steps leading *both* to the formulation of the concept of 'flow' in television *and* to critiques of the concept as either partial or excessively essentialist, Buonanno takes the following turn. 'Without being in any way indifferent to the problems besetting television theory, I should prefer in this book to concentrate on the consequences of the idea of flow for the experience and enjoyment of televisual textuality, and to set out some alternatives based on a phenomenology of viewers' behaviour.' The "both...and" pathway works *both* to examine the complex terrain of the concept *and* to appropriate it as an opening into new territory. Here, as in many other places her 'map' captures the topography of the history of television studies while also exploring the medium anew, from multiple vantage points simultaneously. Approaching the intersections of theory and object in this manner she traces and offers new routes through other concepts as familiar in television studies as flow. 'Glance and gaze', 'media events', 'hybridity and indigenization', 'international flows of media content', – all are crossed and re-crossed.

The structure of the book is itself a version of 'flow'. As concepts are explored they are not left behind, but appear in new places, in new proximate relations to one another. This is made very clear when Buonanno steps into the heated regions surrounding concepts of 'media imperialism'. There she is explicit in her strategy. 'I shall rely on the theories of travel and mobility. Along the way I shall turn the cultural threat into a potential resource and shall finally examine its unequal distribution and manifestations in the contemporary televisual landscape (in this way I shall salvage the media imperialism baby, who does not deserve to be thrown out with the all too abundant bath water.)' The result of such an adventurous new signpost is on the one hand profoundly positive.

> International television flows ('travelling narratives' in my re-definition) can be seen in a new light in the context of this theoretical horizon. We may now be persuaded to consider these flows and re-conceptualize them as *flows of symbolic mobile and mobilizing resources* that have the potential to widen the range of our imaginary geography, multiply our symbolic life-worlds, familiarize ourselves with 'the other' and 'the distant' and construct 'a sense of imagined places': in short, to travel the world and encounter 'otherness' under the protection of the mediated experience. (p. 109)

On the *other* hand, there is no walking away from other crucial implications of the process:

> In conclusion I should like to make it clear that what I regard as a serious problem is neither the centrality of domestic television drama in the panorama of televisual supply (viewers unquestionably need, like and have a right to watch programmes about their own country), nor the presence of the North American product (which is often of excellent quality and not infrequently more innovative and advanced than the domestic product). The problem to be resolved is rather the absence or the marginality of all the other programmes. (p. 116)

Unlike so many studies of television or of specific aspects of the medium, Buonanno's reliance on "both...and" is not an evasion of commitment or precision. Rather, it is a mode of travel that is necessary in constructing this multi-dimensional map, a map that includes both time and space. In the chapter on international flows of media products, for example, she draws not only on her keen critical observation and experience, but on her work as Director of the EuroFiction Project, a multi-year accounting of the production of indigenous fiction in a large number of European countries. 'Data' as well as 'experience' are necessary components in map-making.

But it is ultimately the truly bold experience, the account of risky and dangerous encounters set down by the explorer rather than the tourist that takes this book into its most significant territory. Here I must quote at length in order to capture the profound and beautiful claim made on behalf of this most maligned of media.

> The two great formulae of televisual seriality resort to different temporal subterfuges, but their opposed and complementary 'life strategies' operate by being driven by an identical ambitious project to fulfil our desire to master time: a chimera that never ceases to seduce us with its promise to remove the threat of the ending.

One of the main threads running through this book is the rich potential of 'the multiplying of experiences' that is inherent in television. The considerations addressed in this final chapter suggest an opportunity to integrate the framework, adding that the televisual medium – thanks to the unprecedented volume of serial narrative, structurally predisposed to the exercise of a twofold faculty for dominating time – 'multiplies the experiences of eternity', as Paul Ricoeur says of fictional narrative in general (1988). (p. 132)

If such an assertion seems exaggerated, we can limit ourselves to turning round the banal accusation that is so often levelled at television – that it encourages viewers to escape from or avoid real life – and acknowledge that it displays, on the widest scale known in history, the characteristic that the great serial novelist J R R Tolkien (quoted in Kearney 2002, p. 160) ascribes to popular stories: that they offer a narrative solution to the dilemmas of time and the end and satisfy, with the breathtaking resources of the imagination, the ancient and profound human yearning to achieve the 'Great Flight' – not from life but from death.

Flight from death, survival, aliveness. If coinceived, according to Scannell, as an existential phenomenon that 'refers when all is said and done to being alive, to the survival of our being' (Scannell 2004, p. 141), it is unquestionably true that, by expressing itself on an unprecedented scale and scope, 'liveness' confirms the unique and precious prerogative of the television experience. (p. 132)

In many ways Buonanno's entire study has led us to this point. More than a standard 'argument', the 'flow' of this book, the "both...and" strategy that has enabled rich connectedness, have provided new perspectives on older approaches to many central concerns in the study of television. The large concluding claim cited here builds further on a fundamental conception of the significance of fiction in general. It then links the insights of Barthes, Ricoeur, Gadamer and others to television fiction in particular. There is more here than a commentary on 'form' or 'subject matter'. There is more than a struggle to champion and redeem a medium often dismissed as trivial or meretricious. This is no 'populist salute' to what many would toss away as 'mere entertainment'. In these last pages that emerge so gently yet so powerfully, Milly Buonanno establishes herself as a philosopher of television. She has reached into old reserves of knowledge and experience to report that the new territory is not so strange and threatening after all. Her new map of the terrain of television studies lies like a transparent overlay on some ancient and incomplete drawing of uncharted regions. In keeping with her own observation in the introduction, she demonstrates that new insights do not demolish old ones but build upon and add to them. It is certainly the case that this new work now becomes one of the fundamental texts in television studies, one that should, that must motivate even more explorations by those brave enough to take them.

HN, Athens, Georgia, USA March 2007

1

The Age of Television

Seeing far, going far

1. Transitions

> *A mighty maze of mystic, magic rays*
> *Is all about us in the blue*
> *And in sight and sound they trace*
> *Living pictures out of space*
> *To bring a new wonder to you.*
>
> *...*
>
> *The world is at your door,*
> *It's here to pass you in review*
> *Conjured up in sound and sight*
> *By the magic rays of light*
> *That bring television to you.*[1]

BBC television was transmitted for the first time in November 1936, introduced by the words and music of a celebration piece specially composed for the occasion. This was performed in a romantic interpretation by the singer Adele Dixon (Smith 1995, p. 83). British television was the first in the world to introduce a regular daily television service, even if only for two short hours per day.

The dream-like magic evoked by the inaugural song offers a vivid flavour of the vibrant climate of promise and hopes, hovering between excitement and innocence, in which the new electronic medium made its debut on the world stage in the first half of the twentieth century. Two more decades were to run their course before television, the newest arrival in the era of mass communication, deployed rapidly and on the widest imaginable scale the stunningly magical powers of a 'technology and cultural form' (Williams 1974) that was capable of effecting a profound transformation of human experience. We can accordingly speak of an 'age of television' coinciding with the second half of the twentieth century.

'Age of television' is by no means a misnomer. It is a well-known fact that evolution and the history of the human kind are customarily classified in accordance with time periods; these identify the distinctive characteristics of each epoch by means of a pre-determined factor or a combination of historical and social co-ordinates. Thus we have the Iron Age, the Bronze Age, the classical era and the modern age. The growing development of media of information and communication, together with awareness of the crucial role played by their presence and far-ranging influence in society, has prompted scholars more recently to regard communication itself as an important factor in defining epochs and in distinguishing one from another. 'The history of human existence', Melvin DeFleur and Sandra J. Ball-Rokeach have said in this connection, 'should therefore be more properly explained by a theory of transitions, that is to say *in terms of distinct phases in the development of human communication*' (1995, p. 19).[2] According to the same authors, these distinctive phases can be identified in the transitions from an 'age of signs and signals', going back to the pre-hominids, to an 'age of the spoken word', to the successive ages 'of the written word' and 'of the press', right up to the 'age of mass communications', still running its course while the 'age of computers' is making big strides.

Compared to previous 'ages', the age of mass communications is the shortest so far. It dates from the first decades of the nineteenth century and has thus lasted barely two centuries; yet in that time we have seen four major means of communication come successively into being: the press, the cinema, radio and television. The fact that all four modern forms of mass communication are present and well established in the world of today, alongside more traditional forms of communication (as well as the newest arrivals, the computer and the Internet) clearly demonstrates that these different forms are not substitutes for, but additions to, each other: they co-exist. This cumulative rather than substitutive quality of the course taken by the history of communication is the fundamental lesson imparted by the transitions theory. I am compelled to acknowledge at this point that what I define later on as the 'connective approach' is in large measure a tribute to this lesson, and more generally to a cognitive style that prefers to take co-existence and combinations into consideration (the form 'both...and' or the inclusive distinction) in preference to substitutions or dichotomies (the form 'either...or', or the exclusive distinction; both definitions are taken from Ulrich Beck, 2003, pp. 12–15).

Nevertheless, a new medium tends to edge its predecessors out and install itself in centre stage, since it does not merely join the pre-existing media but reorders the field of play and shakes up existing reciprocal relationships. From this perspective, the epoch of mass communications lends itself to being further subdivided into ages – those of the press, cinema, radio, television – which correspond to the phases when each of the large media assumed a pre-eminent role in the communication system.

As far as television is concerned, its advent and rapid ascent to a leading position in the sphere of information and popular entertainment took place in the second half of the twentieth century. 'Watching TV' then became the main leisure activity for the greater part of the population of the West and ranked third in the order of daily activities, after working and sleeping.

In a relatively limited space of time in terms of the span of history – little more than fifty years – the evolution of the medium has already passed through two clearly distinguishable phases and in recent years has entered a third phase that promises to trigger a major transformation in the world of television as we have hitherto known it. We have all the elements in the brief history of the medium to enable us to further articulate the theory of transitions. I shall dedicate the last part of this chapter to the analysis of the phases of television's development, looked at from a phenomenological and human-centric perspective – a perspective that concentrates on human experience of the medium and, through it, of the world. I shall order my arguments by considering television initially from another starting point: that of the home, this being the environment where television – or rather the object in which it takes shape for public use, namely the apparatus or television set – is firmly ensconced and 'naturalized'.

2. A domesticated medium

Other verses of the song dedicated to television, quoted at the beginning of this chapter, go as follows:

The stars have open eyes that scan us from the skies
And ears that catch the music of the view
They are going to let us share
What they see and hear up there
And show us living pictures from the blue.

In Great Britain, as in the United States, the promotional and advertising material that preceded and accompanied the still experimental beginnings of the new electronic medium from the early part of the twentieth century made great play with its ability to 'bring the world into your own home'. The inaugural song for the BBC transmissions embraced this belief, which from an early stage contributed to the portrayal of television as a medium that was preordained and destined by its nature to be installed and used in the home. 'Television is a domestic medium. It is watched at home. Ignored at home. Discussed at home', claims Roger Silverstone (1994, p. 24). One is unlikely to be mistaken in suggesting that a statement of this kind sounds to most ears so incontrovertible as to risk appearing like a truism – and thus worthy of neither serious discussion nor refutation.

The domestic nature of television, then, is a concept that is taken for granted. It is a given whose presence in various public discussion forums can be traced throughout the historical development of the medium, in diverse formulations according to the events of the moment: the announcement, or forecast, of a transfiguration of the home that is soon to come (*the world is at our door, it's here to pass you in review*), when television was still far from being widely installed in people's homes; the assertion of a *fait accompli* ('Television is a domestic medium'), when television sets have come to be present in nearly all dwellings throughout the planet.

The announcement predates the empirically verifiable and verified reality and therefore takes no account of it. Yet the incontrovertibility of the statement is predicated on this reality. However the announcement and the statement of a *fait accompli* converge in conceiving and asserting this domesticity as an essential prerogative of television, a sort of intangible ontological characteristic.

I intend to question this assumption, not in order to deny the evidence of what is in all senses in front of everyone's eyes – that is to say, the mainly domestic location and use of the television set – but rather to bring back the presumed 'given' of its domestic nature to its true connotation of the 'outcome' of a process. 'Nothing in television's technology determined that it should be a domestic medium', as John Ellis quite rightly observes (2000, p. 31). If television has indeed become a domestic medium, although less exclusively (and probably less definitively) than is believed, this is not because of an imperative that is ineluctably inscribed in the technological nature of the medium, but in consequence of a complex process of installation/incorporation in private living spaces, conceived and adopted from the start as the ideal destination for the television set.

The domesticity of television, in other words, is the product of a 'domestication' of the medium: a domestication that has happened in a relatively short time but not without fears and controversy, nor without a considerable yet barely considered residuum of the small screen's extra-domestic presence. This phase of domestication is very much a thing of the past, largely forgotten by those who witnessed it and unknown to 'television's children', who are too young to remember it and who have grown up in homes where one or more television sets are part of the furniture. Yet this fact should not tempt us to consign this phase to the store-cupboard of things that are superseded and therefore neglected – still less at the present time, when the LCDs of mobile phones seem to bear witness to the avant-garde stage of televisual evolution, opening up the prospect of a television 'set' that can at last be enjoyed away from the domestic space, in public, in the open air, everywhere.

Well, not exactly everywhere; but in public places, not infrequently out of doors in squares, on street corners, in the windows of domestic appliance shops: away from the home is where people all over the world started to enjoy television in the first years of its appearance on the mass media scene. 'In Japan many of the early TV sets were placed not in the home, but on street corners, in front of railway stations and in parks, where large numbers of people gathered. Thus, TV in the mid-1950s was something like an open-air theatre' (Yoshimi 2003, p. 463). In those same years, two-thirds of American families already possessed their own television set, but for the most part 'television was mainly exhibited in public establishments such as taverns, department stores, and even on buses' (Spigel 1992, p.32). In Italy, where a regular transmission service started up in 1954, over ten years were to elapse before half of all families possessed a set; meanwhile bars, taverns, wine bars, clubs, churches and even cinemas were equipped to welcome customers attracted by the new medium. Some viewers, like the peasants of Basilicata observed by Lidia De Rita in a ground-breaking research project into audience ethnography (De Rita 1964), would travel on foot or by bicycle for several miles every evening to get to the only place in their area that had a television set.

So television, in the first phase of its introduction, functioned and was perceived 'as means of encouraging people to *get out at night* (my italics) (Saraceno 2003, p. 2). This offered women in particular unprecedented opportunities for desegregation of domestic spaces and access to company in public places where men spent their free time. Wherever it is found, whether indoors or in open spaces, the enjoyment of television is always a collective experience; one watches it in a group or a small crowd. The news reports at that time described how 'entire families who were previously accustomed to spend their evenings at home now go out: they crowd into the bars and the corner cafés where there is a television set. These places are transformed into little cinemas, little theatres offering both plays and variety shows with chairs arranged informally around the set...' (Dallamano 1955, p. 8, quoted in Sorice 2002, pp. 45–46) In 1958, four years after the arrival of television, it was estimated that there were on average thirty viewers for each television set throughout Italy.

Furthermore the public and collective viewing of television remained a fact even after the small screen arrived in domestic spaces. Particularly at the beginning, but for a number of years so long as having a television set was the exception rather than the rule, families with a set would throw their homes open to relatives, friends and neighbours, welcoming them into the rooms of the home – sitting room, parlour, dining room, breakfast room – where the furniture would be rearranged so as to make room for small seats and 'theatres' with the chairs (sometimes brought along by the guests themselves) arranged in a row or a semi-circle. Television presented its first consumers with an experience of sociability, which was linked in one way or another to a relationship with the outside world. Going to another person's house to watch television in any case means going *outside* one's (own) home, while for the hostess it means allowing a slice of the outside world to come into one's own home in the guise of relative, circle of friends or neighbour. The promise that television 'brings the world into your home' is thus doubly maintained, since the world is brought in not only symbolically through the mediation of the screen but concretely through the open door that welcomes people and things coming from *outside*.

The fascinating studies by Cecelia Tichi (1991) and more especially by Lynn Spigel (1992) reconstructed the transformation of the home into a 'home theatre' in post-war America, when owning a television set became an integral part of an ideal of family life, built on a complex relationship between privatization and connection of the domestic with the public sphere. 'The ideology of privacy was not experienced simply as a retreat from the public sphere; it also gave people a sense of belonging to the community' (Spigel 1992, pp. 100–101). Television, being able to connect the internal with the external, the nuclear family with the extended network of neighbours, home life with social circle, chimes in perfectly with this ideal and is also its precise epitome.

The arrival of television in the home – which, it must be re-stated, did not equate straight away to a loss, still less a final loss, of its collective character of public viewing – nevertheless provoked worry, anxieties and discontent, in Italy as elsewhere. In this connection, Andrea Press has collected the reminiscences of adult American women who, recalling the 1950s, testified to their ambivalent reactions towards the introduction of television into the home: they thought 'that it was a wonderful thing' (Press 1991, p. 54) but at the same time they were sorry to have to renounce the nights out and the life away from home that they had previously enjoyed as emancipated young women. In open disagreement with Joshua Meyrowitz's thesis (1985), which identifies television – since it brought about a symbolic rift with the historical segregation of women in domestic spaces – as one of the key factors in generating feminism, Lynn Spigel records and sustains the fears, echoed by some sectors of the popular media at that time, that women risked being further confined to their homes (Spigel 1992, p. 215).

Other fears were aroused by the friendly and sociable custom of welcoming groups into the home to watch television. The 'electronic neighbourhood' that gathered in homes with a television set may on the one hand have helped to strengthen ties within the group – causing that group, furthermore, to be a witness and a beneficiary of the affluence of the proprietors and of their 'up-to-the-minute' openness to the latest entertainment technology. But it may possibly on the other hand have constituted an unwelcome and threatening intrusion into intimate family life. The outside world brought in by television, by means of the twofold access through screen and front door, seemed to many to be as much a potential peril as 'a wonderful thing'.

A few weeks before Italian television came into being, the renowned journalist Arrigo Benedetti published an article in *La nuova stampa* entitled 'Television and its ghosts' (1953, p. 3). The ghosts in this instance were metaphorical and did not allude to anything paranormal: the author was replying to an earlier article by the writer Paolo Monelli, who was very pessimistic about the imminent advent of television. But a strong current of anxiety towards the presence of television in the home was reinforced over a long period by a genuine association of the new electronic medium with occult and extraterrestrial phenomena. Jeffrey Sconce (2000) has carried out a truly original study of 'electronic ghosts'. This study documents the rise and the manifestation (disseminated in many texts of popular appeal: let *Poltergeist* by Steven Spielberg be the best example of the genre) of a horrifying and almost paranoid fantasy that attributes to the medium (in itself a word that evokes paranormal phenomena) sinister forces that are inherent in its technology. Television has been demonized and feared on account of a range of horrors, from its malignant ability to observe and control the occupants of the house (already prefigured in George Orwell's dystopic novel *1984*) that changes the happy proclamation of the song

> *The stars have open eyes that scan us from the skies*
> *And ears that catch the music of the view*

into an anxiety-inducing alarm call, to the terrifying power to suck the living into a universe of oblivion outside space and time (*Poltergeist*); to the distressing literal fulfilment of the promise to transport viewers through space and time to the place where what they see on the screen is happening (a fear echoed in 1950s sci-fi and in the more recent film *Pleasantville*). According to Sconce, 'television remains, even forty years after its introduction into the American home, a somewhat unsettling and alien technology' (Sconce 2000, p. 165).

All this did not prevent the spread of the completely opposite belief of a technological object so docile and serviceable (but also inert and passive) that it could be confused with the other electrical appliances in the house: not much more than 'a toaster with pictures' (McCarthy 2001, p. 117). Ranking the television set no higher than any domestic appliance is still one of the most self-satisfied and popular clichés; and it is probably the one that emphasizes to the greatest extent – as a statement of the obvious or an irreversible point of no return – television's 'domestification'. 'As far as I know, there's no climate of cultural criticism directed at the fridge' was the ironic comment of John Hartley (1999, p. 104), concerning the unlikely equivalence of television set and refrigerator.

In reality, television has never become a completely domesticated medium, or a totally domesticated and domestic material object, however much an affirmation of this kind clashes with common sense (including the common sense that is scientifically credited). Not merely because its presence, even though it has become part of the geography of inhabited space, continues to cause alarm, suspicion and the surveillance kept for things that one knows cannot entirely be trusted (and again, nothing like that happens with fridges or dishwashers); but also because television sets and screens have never in fact abandoned the public spaces that they originally occupied; rather, they have continued to spread exponentially in areas outside the home during and after the phase of domestication.

Thanks to the growing interconnection between media studies and theories of social spaces, we are aware of an extensive diffusion of what Anna McCarthy (2001), in her ground-breaking work that is already considered authoritative, has defined as 'ambient television', or television outside the home. Bars and hotels, prisons and hospitals, stations and airports, trade centres, waiting rooms and other waiting and transit areas: television screens are omnipresent in many different extra-domestic places. Here television displays the versatility of a site-specific apparatus: contextualized, capable of blending (to the point of our being unaware of it, but not necessarily spoiling our equally contextualized viewing) with widely diverse situations in everyday life – both at home and elsewhere.

3. A dual sense of place

'Each time we use the word "television", we actually commemorate one of the signal novelties of this technology: its capacity to allow us to see (-vision) at a distance (tele-)' (Allen, 2004, p. 105).

Seeing at a distance, seeing far: the etymological meaning of the word may be entirely syntonic with a McLuhanesque conception of the media as an extension of our senses (in this instance the sense of vision), but the experience of television turns out to be richer and more complex than a simple extension of the range of one's gaze. It is this which makes the *doyenne* of televisual metaphors – 'a window on the world' – inadequate, if appealing. In actual fact 'watching television', although commonly expressed in terms that in accordance with its etymology underline the primacy of vision, does not equate solely to experiencing a (symbolically) enhanced faculty of sight, that from the viewer's location is focused on the horizons of far-off worlds, bringing them to the nearness of the screen. Watching television also resembles an experience of displacement, of moving away, of mobility, which is accomplished or rather 'takes place' in the framework of the dynamic relationship between the localized context of the place where the television is watched (mostly, as we know, in the home) and the distant contexts where, for their part, the events seen on screen are taking place. Thus 'watching television' corresponds not only to seeing far, but also and perhaps above all to 'going far'.

'Going far' thus means away from home, since it is normally at home that we watch television. The ambivalence of the relationship between internal and external, inside and outside, that characterizes (as we have seen) the process of introducing the television set into private living spaces, is here reproduced in the phenomenology of a symbolic and imaginary departure, favoured by the same medium that so to speak 'colonized' those spaces. This confirms the resistance of television to being conceptually and empirically confined, completely and definitively, within the four walls of the home. These walls have become in a certain sense porous, or like sliding doors, so as to allow a two-way traffic of the outside world coming in and the imaginative experience going out.

It is quite easy to come to believe that one is seeing in this two-way traffic a game, largely mechanical if the truth be told, of opposing symmetries: on the one hand the privatizing of what is public (the entry of the outside world into the domestic sphere); on the other hand the publicizing of what is private (domestic consumption migrates into the public sphere). In reality, as Anna McCarthy rightly observes, 'public spaces are not purely and self-evidently public; they are, like every other cultural space, characterised by particular configurations of public and private' (McCarthy 2001, p. 121). If anything, it is a case of recognizing that television, as a material object and a cultural experience, changes and remodels this particular configuration to a significant degree.

Inherent in the much vaunted promise to offer viewers the hyper-realistic sense of 'being there', right on the spot where the events are taking place, rather than an illusion of reality, the concept of a symbolic and imaginative mobility connected with the televisual experience has been advanced and revisited fairly regularly in television studies and in related discursive contexts – though without ever acquiring the importance that it deserves. Already in the 1950s Daniel Lerner, in a study of modernization in the Middle East, had perceived with foresight the capacity of the media to be a 'mobility multiplier' (quoted in Thompson 1995, p. 211). Some decades later, developing an analogy between television and the means of transport that had previously been seized upon by Rudolph Arnheim (Morse 1990, p. 193), Ben Bachmair upheld the functional equivalence between the motor car and television, and traced the rapid spread of both machines (one mechanical, the other electronic) back to the reciprocal and organic consonance with a more general cultural model of encouraging individual mobility. 'Television succeeded because it broadened and extended lifestyles associated with the motor-car: primarily those concerned with mobility as a shaping principle of communication' (Bachmair 1991, p. 522). Watching television, observes Anna McCarthy when introducing the theme of travel (which I shall address in detail in chapter VII), gives one the 'sense of travel to another place' (2001, p. 137).

Raymond Williams (1974, 1992) was, however, one of the first to grasp the close correlation between television and mobility, and to build it into the concept of 'mobile privatization'. Williams coined the phrase in the context of a discussion on the apparently contradictory, but in fact interconnected, aspects of modern social life as it had been evolving since the beginning of the Industrial Revolution. On the one hand, the housing and production structures of the integrated communities and settlements of pre-modern society were being uprooted; on the other hand, there was a compelling need to maintain social contacts between the dismembered family unit and the outside world, now much larger, distant and complex. An ideal of domestic privacy co-exists with the crucial need not to be cut off from the world; the family who appear to be self-sufficient acknowledge the need as well as the desire 'to go out and see new places' (1992, p. 20). Television perfects the process started by radio broadcasting and thus – argues Williams – resolves the contradiction, in that it allows people to 'to go out and see new places' without moving physically from their homes.

Going far away, mobility, going round the world while staying at home at the same time (*Home and Away*, to quote the title of an Australian soap that is also very popular outside its country of origin): all the evidence points to the fact that we are dealing with the experience of space and the power of television to transform it.

In this connection, I intend to address the problem posed by the assumption that television generates a 'delocalization' of social life: or, to use Joshua Meyrowitz's (1985) undeniably more attractive and vivid turn of phrase, 'no sense of place'. I should like to consider it from a new standpoint, as I have done above for the concept of domesticity: a standpoint on which I have already made some preliminary observations emphasizing the dislocative aspects of television viewing. Meyrowitz is the author of a famous and important study, published in the mid-1980s under the title *No Sense of Place*. This ambitious study, which has become a classic, has substantially increased our awareness and understanding of the televisual medium: it manages to combine the macro-sociological 'medium theory' approach advanced by Marshall McLuhan and Harold Innis – the founding fathers of communications studies – with the micro-sociology of social interaction developed by Erving Goffman according to a dramaturgical model. At the heart of the author's analytical arguments we find the compelling idea that the electronic media distort what he defines as 'the situational geography' of social life: we are present at events without being on the place and communicate with other people without meeting them in the flesh. In the past, physical location was the main determinant of social situations; now it is disassociated or 'divorced' from the social location, since 'where we are physically no longer determines where and who we are socially' (1985, p. 115). Meyrowitz provides a wealth of examples, including what he himself describes as the extreme case of prisons, to demonstrate how access to the outside world by means of television weakens the grip of physical location on our experience and behaviour. Meyrowitz's arguments are peppered with felicitous and incisive language, such as the much-quoted statement that 'television...now escorts children across the globe even before they have permission to cross the street'. (p. 238).

Meyrowitz's thinking is daringly innovative; his arguments often reveal his strong convictions. One cannot say the same, however, about the conclusion that he reaches which, summarized in his title, clearly marks out the interpretative framework of the whole work: the weakening or loss of the sense of place, the 'de-localization' of social life. 'When we are everywhere', affirms the author, 'we are also no place in particular' (p. 125).

In fact watching television is not the same as being everywhere and therefore nowhere in particular. Watching television equates to an experience of mobility and dislocation between diverse places – one of them physical and one social if one wishes to conserve Meyrowitz's distinction – rather than the removal or indeterminacy of the place (one is reminded of the overworked concept of no-place, as well as the *nowhere* of televisual dystopia). These diverse places do not cancel each other out, but interact within the new co-existence between nearness and distance, here and elsewhere, home and world, 'home and away'.

We find enlightening thoughts about this in the work of Paddy Scannell, a prominent English scholar. Scannell (1996), whose writings have been taken up by other writers, has made explicit the idea that television and radio 'create new possibilities of being: of *being in two places at once*' (my italics) (Scannell 1996, p. 91). These are the only two places in the world where most people live, according to what literary intuition caused Don deLillo to say in *White Noise* (1985), sometimes quoted at the head of writings about television: 'For most people there are only two places in the world. Where they live and their TV set' (quoted in Tichi 1991, *no page number*).

Television's most significant impact on the spatial experience of present-day individuals rests – in Scannell's observation, which one can share – in the simultaneousness of being and feeling oneself here and elsewhere, thus with a dual sense of place. It is much less a 'divorce' between physical and social place that is perpetrated in this impact, than a creation of conditions of bigamy or a 'polygamy of place', which Ulrich Beck (2003, p. 59) sees as one more characteristic of global modernity.

The dual sense of place reappears in the multiplicity of experiential possibilities that are promoted, in the words of Giddens, by the 'openness of the world to the individual' (1991, p. 189). The electronic media have helped to expand this opening, through which the remote and foreign are insinuated into the near and familiar, bringing about a new kind of experience of place marked by the ambivalent relationship between presence and absence, nearness and distance, localization and dislocalization. So it is, according to Giddens, that the place – permeated by distant influences – becomes like a dream or a phantom (1994, p. 30), in the dual meaning of a jumble of bright sounds and images and a mysterious apparition. That definition embraces both magic and ghosts, conspiring to place television in an ambivalent relationship between the wondrous and the ordinary.

4. Broadcasting and narrowcasting
Recognizing that the domestic nature of television is an elaborate historical and cultural construct allows us to underline the public and collective dimension of television – in its guises that change according to the context – just as our discussion of the sense of place have revealed the part played by simultaneousness in the specifically bi-local experience of television. Both these concepts will prove to be useful later, when we pursue our initial discussion on the television age and its internal stages of evolution.

I have already referred in this connection to a triple division of time periods. Dividing the history of the medium into three phases is the practice of several present-day scholars (for American television, see, for example, Rogers, Epstein, Reeves 2002), even though the specific nature of national histories and the criteria used for identification can suggest different ways of dividing up time in different cases.

John Ellis (2000) recently proposed a three-way division that has aroused a great deal of interest and support in the field of international television studies. It is based on what might be defined as 'the growing volume of what is available'; in other words, the progressive extension and multiplication of the channels and contents offered to the viewing public. I propose to summarize Ellis's thesis rapidly in order to provide a starting point for some additional observations, and in particular to introduce an opposing viewpoint that is more coherent and consistent with what I have argued up to this point.

Ellis defines the first phase of the age of television, starting with the period of its origin until (roughly) the second half of the 1970s or the beginning of the 1980s, as a phase of *scarcity*: it is characterized by the existence of a limited number of channels, and by an equally limited number of hours of transmission per day. In Italy, as in other European countries, the initial phase of the television age coincided with the public service monopoly. At the beginning there was only one national terrestrial channel; many years were to pass before it was joined by a second and, much later, by a third network.

The next period started with the arrival of commercial television, in the transition from the 1970s to the 1980s. This was a phase of *growth*: a relatively wide and varied choice of channels and programmes became available for viewers and the competition for audience ratings became more intense. Viewers were spread out in varying degrees within the widest range of the distribution system (in Italy the national networks increased from two to six, bringing the addition of vast numbers of local networks in their train).

The third phase got under way in the course of the 1990s, at varying rates of progress in different countries. This was the phase of *abundance*. Thanks to cable, satellite and digital technologies that were often combined or synergetic, it witnessed the multiplication of channels by a factor of ten or even a hundred; the diversification of the modes of accessing the programmes; the distribution of those programmes on a variety of platforms and networks; and the concomitant tendency towards segmentation of the viewing public. The third phase of the television age coincides with what is customarily defined as the multi-channel environment.

Although Ellis offers us in this way an accurate and useful contribution to the ordering of developments in television over the half-century and more of the medium's history, the fact that he gives prominence to the distribution system places his reconstruction within the dynamics of 'magnificent and progressive' expansion, which risks overshadowing aspects that are more static or that do not travel along the direct route from scarcity to abundance. If the number of channels seems infinitely expandable, thanks to transmission by cable and above all by digital technology (see chapter IV), other very important dimensions do not evolve in the same direction. For example, the infinite elasticity of the distributive spectrum is offset by the inelasticity of the time available for watching television; we are talking about a substantial slice of daily time that in some societies and social segments (the elderly) can reach and exceed four hours, but which – wherever television has reached a extensive level of penetration – tends to stabilize around a threshold that resists further encroachment, however many television programmes may be on offer.

The abundance of channels is furthermore accompanied by a relative scarcity of content; indeed it is the cause of such inadequacy. The need, not always easily met, for a huge number of programmes of all genres to fill up the time slots of the numerous television channels was already evident during the growth phase. But in the multi-channel environment the need for programmes increases exponentially, giving rise among other things to a particular phenomenon: the incorporation of the history of the medium in the more advanced forms of its present. The lack of a sufficient quantity of new material – owing to the scarcity of both money and ideas – creates the conditions for extensive recourse to archive material and old television programmes in order to feed, in whole or in part, the voracious appetite of a distribution system that is expanding at an enormous rate. Neither the press nor radio nor cinema feed off their own past, except on rare occasions; television is the only one of the large media to set up a living museum of itself.

Furthermore, the horizon of televisual abundance opens up boundless territories, but these are not freely and unconditionally accessible: on the contrary. The cable and satellite networks which crowd our multi-channel environment indicate a transition in the way people access their television, compared to what happened in the previous phase. This is the passage from free television to television by subscription. Although only commercial television is totally free of charge, the form of payment demanded by nearly all the public networks – an annual rental

– has never constituted, in the strict sense, an unavoidable key to accessing television transmissions, nor is it perceived as such; one can evade paying the rental and still watch the public networks. It is on the other hand impossible (except in cases of piracy) to access payment channels without paying the subscription and buying or hiring the technology that enables one to receive the transmission.

Television with and without subscription co-exist within the same televisual systems and the same multi-channel households. It is reasonable to believe that a sizeable proportion of the population will continue to enjoy free television for economic and cultural reasons, whether from preference or necessity. Access by subscription has, however, brought about a significant change in the history and collective perception of television. On an equal footing with radio – but taking advantage of the extra resource associated with a polysensorial medium (words and pictures) as well as enjoying a central position in the communications system – television has distinguished itself historically by its low threshold of accessibility, helped by the fact of being free of charge. Listening to the radio or watching television requires no prior acquisition of competencies – you have to be literate to read books and newspapers and using the Internet requires further technological literacy – nor any acquisitive act that has to be repeated from time to time, like buying a newspaper or a cinema ticket. Easily accessible and user-friendly television is without doubt the most democratic of the large media, as Meyrowitz repeatedly underlines. The evolution towards television by subscription therefore represents a clear break, practical and symbolic, with the previously unfettered open-door aspect of the medium.

In the end – but the caveat applies whatever temporal criterion one chooses to adopt – we must bear in mind that transitions from scarcity to abundance should not be understood as being on a par with mutually exclusive phases; it is better understood if one adopts an approach which is, so to speak, connective rather than substitutive. In the greater part of the contemporary television scene the most recent phases of the evolution of the medium co-exist in various ways with the earlier ones: not only because of a 'question of time', and thus the more or less advanced stage of the process of change, but also because change, in every sphere of a complex society, manifests itself and settles down in a cumulative and stratified pluralization and diversification of what is 'available', instead of in a substitution of the old by the new as inexorable as it is restrictive (as the transitions theory teaches us). This applies in particular when the new raises the threshold of access. Hardly anyone lives any more in a regime of televisual scarcity; yet even in the most televisually developed countries only a part of the population – even if it is growing, at rates varying between one context and another – enjoys a regime of abundance.

My clarifications are not intended to cast doubt on the legitimacy and relevance of Ellis's choice of criteria, nor of the usefulness of the reconstruction that these criteria allow us to make. I identify rather in this reconstruction a valuable canvas providing the background on which I can sketch out what from my own perspective (that of experience, and the relevance of experience in the televisual field) emerges as the most important and significant transition to be observed in television's history. I am referring to the passage from broadcasting to narrowcasting, or in other words from generalist to specialised television (or thematic, to use the more current but less precise expression).

Although this is an entirely orthodox and indeed conventional way of looking at the historical evolution of the medium, I want to emphasize at once how opting for the transition from broadcasting to narrowcasting is not merely a device for saying in different words what can equally be said in terms of the passage from scarcity to abundance. On the contrary, it is a complete reversal of perspective, since the dynamic of expansion that drives the path to abundance turns out to be exactly reversed: that is to say, it becomes a dynamic of contraction made crystal clear in the terminology itself, which indicates the sequential passage of broad televisual diffusion (to the widest possible audience) to a narrow diffusion (to smaller sections of the public).

We can say 'diffusion', or perhaps better 'dissemination', at any rate when referring to broadcasting. At first glance it seems strange to have recourse to an expression taken from a traditional agricultural dictionary to describe the functioning of a means of communication which (if nothing else initially) has strong connotations of modern urbanity. The word 'broadcasting' originally indicated the act of scattering seeds in large handfuls by a sower over a wide area of tilled earth. Yet this is how the dissemination of television functions, as John Durham Peters (1999) explains to us in one of the most profound and thoughtful books about communication ever written. Peters' main concern is to rescue broadcasting from the widespread and persistent criticism that, in setting it against an idealized and almost sacrosanct model of interactive dialogue, blames it for the bad influences of a form of communication that is supposedly undemocratic because it is a one-way monologue. Instead Peters, without attempting to set one theory against another or establish that either is superior, compares the communicative models of dialogue and dissemination and traces them back respectively to the great moral figures of Socrates and Jesus. His purpose is to demonstrate that 'dialogue can be tyrannical and dissemination can be just' (1999, p. 34). In particular Peters draws inspiration from the Gospel parable of the sower to put forward a persuasive argument for the non-selective, one might say ecumenical, nature of broadcasting. As the parable teaches us, the sower has no control over the harvest; or, in the terms of a media studies jargon, no control over the reception context. Like the seeds, which can fall on stony ground, or be eaten by birds, or blown far away by the wind, so that only some of them fall on good ground, televisual dissemination goes out indiscriminately in all directions and is 'democratically indifferent' to the uncontrolled randomness of its effects and consequences. 'The parable of the sower,' says Peters, 'celebrates broadcasting as an equitable mode of communication' (1999, p. 52).

The first phase of the television age (and, to a lesser extent, the second as well) is thus marked by the establishment of broadcasting, in the guise of terrestrial and subscription-free generalist television. By virtue of its wide accessibility, generalist television spread rapidly and revealed an unparalleled capacity for reaching huge audiences at the same time; also for bringing together whole nations, for special ceremonial events of various types, several countries and even the whole world (Dayan and Katz, 1993, see chapter III)). The capacity to attract mass audiences was naturally never as great as it had been in the phase of distributive spectrum scarcity, when the smaller number of available networks was in itself a powerful factor in aggregating audiences. But broadcasting, if only in conditions of greater competitiveness, has shown itself to be effective in retaining substantial audiences even in the later phases of the system's growth and to this day, as in Italy where the generalist terrestrial networks maintain the greater market share.

Bringing together audiences is in fact the purpose and function of broadcasting; and since – contrary to what is widely believed as common sense – large aggregates of individuals (inaccurately defined as the masses) show a high degree of internal heterogeneity rather than homogeneity, it is in the context of communication with many different viewers that generalist television is measured. This entails work mainly on what is shared or can be shared among heterogeneous subjects by gender, age, education, lifestyle and other attributes. In order to attract audiences numbering millions, generalist television has to appeal to an aggregate component of diverse segments of the population. The concept of programming inherent in broadcasting 'effectively puts into practice an acceptance of the heterogeneity of tastes and aspirations and thus constitutes a sort of recognition of their equality' (Wolton 1990, p. 115).[3]

The orientation of broadcasting in order to bring together the widest range of viewers, understood by many to be no more than a simple quest for the lowest common denominator, has performed and continues to perform important functions of culture and identity binding within the national collectivity of each country. Television itself has helped to construct this collectivity symbolically, offering it a non-physical meeting place where participants may experience mutual visibility and recognition. Generalist television has served to forge a shared 'imagination' of the national community, with considerably more impact and above all to a far greater extent compared to the press (Anderson 1991); in Italy its effect has been among other things a primary force in linguistic unification, anticipating the process of universal schooling (Bechelloni 1984, 1995).

Mentioning the community at this point allows us to tidy up a few loose ends in our discussion of the televisual experience. We have observed the collective ways in which television was watched, as much outside the home as within it, in the early years of the new medium; and we have identified, in the privilege of being simultaneously in two places, the specific point about television. This sense of a collective and simultaneous vision is a constant accompaniment of television-watching; it is an experience of connecting, and sharing broader or narrower circles, with other individuals and viewers.

In this context Daniel Dayan wrote: 'Watching television is always a collective exercise, even when one is alone in front of the set (2001, p. 743). Watching television means 'watching with'; watching with all the other distant and unknown viewers whom one supposes or guesses 'are simply there' in front of their screens at the same time as we are in front of ours, watching the same programme or part of a programme that we are watching ourselves. The same programme at the same moment; the 'invisible meeting' evoked by television consists of a double sharing, on the part of the viewing public, of a symbolic material and of the time spent on enjoying it. It is important to distinguish between different types of simultaneousness. The one that is embraced by the experience of 'watching with' is not the synchronization with the real time of a live event, shot and followed live (for more on 'liveness', see chapter III), but the synchronization between individuals who are far apart and unknown to each other but who are doing, and know that they are doing, the same thing at the same time. It is a form of 'despatialised simultaneity' (Thompson, 1995, p. 32), entirely analogous with the simultaneous or nearly simultaneous reading of the daily newspaper. On this point, Benedict Anderson says: 'Each communicant is well aware that the ceremony he performs is being replicated simultaneously by thousands (or millions) of others of whose existence he is confident, yet of whose identity he has not the slightest notion' (Anderson 1991, p. 35).

The concept of community must be approached with great caution when one is speaking of vicarious experiences. But one can affirm, limiting oneself explicitly to the word's general sense of togetherness, that watching television means entering into a connection and being aware of it even in a latent and unnoticed way, with the imagined community – intangible, scattered and ephemeral though it may be – of all those who are watching it at the same moment.

The imagined communities, or the invisible meeting of simultaneous viewers of the same programme, make up aggregates that are changeable in terms of scale and internal composition; and that changeability, among other things, has something to do with the forms and directions taken by television development. In the most triumphal phase of broadcasting, watching television was similar to participating in a viewers' community that was not only enormous but, still more important in the matter of social links, was characterized by the 'internal pluralism' of the heterogeneous representation of different components of collectivity, brought together by the ecumenical communicative model of dissemination. In time, initially in the transition to the second phase of broadcasting – a phase open to the growing availability of still generalist channels, but already veering towards a differentiation inspired by competitive logic – watching television has become an experience, above all with the advent of narrowcasting, that is shared within more restricted social circles that are at the same time more homogeneous in their internal structure, brought together by a selective communication model. One meets up basically in a small group of equals rather than a large group of disparate people.

Narrowcasting – in concrete terms, the proliferating system of minority channels and small cable and satellite networks available on subscription – certainly reflects the distributive abundance brought about by technological evolution. But it would be proof of one's technological determinism not to acknowledge that the advent of narrowcasting has also been made possible by the emergence of a strain of social demand, not widespread but diffused to a greater or lesser degree according to the particular case, for 'made-to-measure' television tailored to the specific preferences and interests of a restricted number of viewers (the so-called 'niche' market): a demand that the generalist broadcasting networks are evidently not in a position to satisfy.

As narrowcasting has appeared on the scene and become widespread (very unevenly in some countries' television systems as compared to others), the enduring substitutive viewpoint that has prevailed in discussions about the media and its processes of change has expressed itself all too easily in declarations, predictions and expectations concerning the imminent demise of broadcasting. While one can confine oneself to saying that this is not so, and (plausibly) not merely because it is a 'question of time', it is more useful to reflect on the logics of the opposing and complementary functioning of broadcasting and narrowcasting.

On the one hand generalist television with its diverse range of programmes aimed at an equally diverse range of audiences, by reason of the extent of its catchment area, is committed to keeping together and thus to bringing about a 'recomposition' of audiences into some sort of commonality (of interests, pleasures, viewing choices etc.). On the other hand specialized television, with its numerous channels offering monovalent programmes with a specific theme, tries to bring about a 'decomposition' of the heterogeneous into the homogeneous, carving out restricted and uniform segments from the wide range of audiences and subject matter and keeping them within a regime of reciprocal 'separateness'. Each network has its speciality, its conclave of viewers, its topics that occupy a large or a small niche. The vast audience united in front of the screen by a typical generalist programme aimed at families would, if confronted by narrowcasting, be split into fragments by an assortment of networks bent on giving (or so it is promised) everyone what they need, without any limit: cartoons for the children, sport for the fans, films for film lovers, documentaries for nature lovers, recipes for those who like cooking, and much else.

Narrowcasting, then, is divisive and selective, just as broadcasting joins and unifies people. The former isolates and separates, the latter unites people and keeps them together. Let us suppose, as a purely conjectural hypothesis, that broadcasting were to be scaled down to a mere residual presence: in such an event we ought to be seriously concerned at the disappearance of a symbolic space in which it has been possible for the public to meet up in various ways as different parts of the same community, at the moments when those parts come together as an audience of viewers, or indeed as performers on generalist television. If the city is the place where one can meet different people, then – to take the widely used metaphor of the town square – generalist television should be consciously regarded a having an urban connotation. By contrast, the metaphor of the club (or circle, or association, or any place specifically for gatherings of people with shared interests, passions or ideals) is perhaps more fitting to denote the narrowcasting networks.

Narrowcasting (like dialogue, which incidentally it is considered to resemble) has the benefit of positive prejudice which considers it to be 'a superior form of television, compared to the generalist' (Wolton 1990, p. 119)[4] – probably because of the progressive 'aura' emanating from the new technology. Sometimes it is acknowledged with the supreme redeeming compliment of not even being television. As a matter of fact, broadcasting is no more conservative than narrowcasting is progressive and, taking a cue from John Durham Peters, one could say that if the first can be unbiased, the second can be discriminatory.

But in the end, if we abandon the competitive field that aims to declare winners and losers between broadcasting and narrowcasting, we shall see well how town squares and clubs, generalism and specialism, commonality and separateness, dissemination and dialogue can and must be truly destined to exist side by side in the worlds of television that we now inhabit.

Notes
1. Lyrics written by James Dyrenforth; music composed by Kenneth Leslie-Smith. Reproduced here and in section 2 of this chapter by kind permission of the BBC Written Archives Centre, Caversham Park, Reading.
2. Translated from Italian: 'La storia dell'esistenza umana dovrebbe quindi essere spiegata più opportunamente da una teoria delle transizioni, vale a dire *in termini di fasi distintive dello sviluppo della comunicazione umana*' (translator's note).
3. Translated from French: 'Elle traduit de ce fait une acceptation de l'hétérogeneité de goûts et des aspirations et constitue donc une sorte de reconnaissance de leur égalité' (translator's note).
4. Translated from French: 'L'idée qui fait de la télévision fragmentée une forme de télévision supérieure par rapport à la télévision généraliste' (translator's note).

2

Theories of the Medium
Flow, glance, gaze

1. Multiple conceptions of television

'Hence television is a somewhat difficult object, unstable, all over the place, tending derisively to escape anything we can say about it: given the speed of its changes...its interminable flow... its quantitative everydayness...how can we *represent* television?' (Heath 1990, p.267) Stephen Heath asked this question in the closing essay of one of the most important collections of theoretical contributions on television (*The Logic of Television*) published in the past twenty years. Although this sort of question may seem quite senseless to those – perhaps no less numerous today than at the beginning of the1990s – who consider television to be too unsophisticated and commonplace, it is entirely true that its complicated and multi-faceted configuration of 'technology and cultural form' (Williams 1974, 1992) presents an ongoing challenge to the intellectual task of representing it.

As a 'somewhat difficult object', television lends itself to being looked at from differing theoretical viewpoints, as will be demonstrated below: each of these investigates, analyses and tries to explain the various aspects of the medium's nature. This type of division of theoretical labour can hardly be avoided but is entirely legitimate, intellectually economical and effective in simplifying complexity; the problem, or a source of confusion, lies if anywhere in the absence of forms of recognition and thematization of the range of approaches. All this happens often, as if the individual and partial theoretical perspectives were to restore an integral representation of the televisual medium, whereas they are the result of a selection – almost never stated – carried out both in the field of the many possible approaches and in the wide range of possible questions inherent in each approach. '...general recognition of differences between *kinds of theory* about television needs to be much clearer and more explicit than it often has been ', John Corner states in this connection (Corner 1997, p. 259), after having explained and examined a typology of theories to which I shall return later.

In the same vein, Joshua Meyrowitz has drawn up a typology of three major metaphorical constructs (Meyrowitz 1993,1998), which in his opinion represent the main ways of seeing and conceiving the nature of television (and of the media in general):

a. The metaphor of the *channels*. This is by far the most common metaphor in collective perception, if only because it coincides with the first thing that everyone experiences when using diverse means of communication. The metaphor, which refers to the channelling and conveying of flows of symbolic material, raises questions such as: What are the contents? What social, political, economic, organizational, ideological or other factors have influenced its evolution and perception? To what extent do the contents of television reflect real life? How do the various audiences interpret it? What effect does it have on them? The succession of waves of alarm concerning the media, and above all television, can, for example, be attributed to this metaphorical construct, which amongst other characteristics is indifferent to the structural specificity of individual media. Take the case of programmes containing violence; points of view will vary greatly according to whether the violence is to be found in discussions and representations in the cinema, television or the press; but the difference in each case is lost if one assigns to the cinema, television and the press the same nature and function of a mere channel and vehicle for the contents.

b. The metaphor of *language*. This second metaphor focuses on the grammar and aesthetics of the media, and puts questions that concern the manipulation of grammar variables (the perspectives and movements of the camera, spatial and temporal frameworks, visual compositions, sound effects and much else); their influence in terms of perception, comprehension or the emotional reaction of audiences; the cultural or ideological factors that favour the choice of determined codes; and the contribution made by the grammar rules to the presentation and construction of the content. One is reminded of the scene in *Citizen Kane*, Orson Welles's masterpiece, when Kane's second wife, an abysmally bad singer exposed to devastatingly negative criticisms, implores him to allow her to abandon the stage; cowering at first on the carpet, surrounded by copies of the daily papers in which she has read about the irrevocable failure of her own ambitions, she gets up on her knees and is gradually covered by the overwhelming shadow of Kane, who is otherwise not visible, forcing her to go on performing. It is one example among many others of the enormous and meaningful importance of the language of the media, which explains the priority or the exclusive attention to the linguistic dimension that characterizes some perspectives of the studio (in truth, this can be verified much more in the context of film than that of television studies).

c. The metaphor of the *environment*. The third construct refers to a conception of the media as a set of contexts with specific structural characteristics, different for each medium, which transcend those same content- and language-related components. The metaphor of the environment, which as we have noted inspired the works of Meyrowitz (1993) and recalls the medium theory of which the main exponents are the founding fathers of communication studies such as Harold Innis and Marshall McLuhan, prompts questions of the following type: Which economic, political or social factors promote the development of a medium that possesses certain characteristics, compared to other media with different characteristics? To what extent does the advent of a new medium change the functions and modalities of the use of existing media? What repercussions do a medium's characteristics have on its contents, language and the way it is enjoyed? For example, it is on the basis of the metaphor of environment that Meyrowitz argues how television has contributed to the liberation of women, even when presenting contents that are undeniably sexist; the specific structural characteristics of television have in fact allowed women to escape from the spatial, informative and social segregation that was inflicted on them in patriarchal society.

Each of the conceptions of television's nature that is summed up in the three metaphorical constructs provides material for studies, analyses and research whose findings can be relied upon 'in their own terms'. But to ignore or disregard the fact that studies and results are produced within the confines of a pre-determined vision, excluding all others (at least in most cases), induces one to pass over in silence the selection processes that govern every specific approach. It also compels one to establish a fictitious competition between acquisitions that would otherwise lend themselves to being considered complementary and supplementary to each other, and whose apparent contradictoriness refers to the fact that they stem from different conceptions and different levels of analysis. It can thus happen that an analysis of the content of a certain genre of television programmes can lead to the conclusion that women are portrayed in a demeaning or misogynistic light; but a structural analysis of the same programmes could instead suggest a different or opposite conclusion, as happens not infrequently in the cinema (many 'dark lady' figures, incarnations of a phobic feminine myth, turn out to be highly praised in terms of film language). An analysis, for its part, of television as environment draws attention to the fact that as well as the contents and language of specific programmes, television in itself breaks away from separation of the sexes and puts women in contact and relationship with areas that were exclusively male in the past.

At first glance all this risks giving the impression that 'great is the confusion' in the world of television studies. This impression may have been reinforced by the fact that there are more theoretical approaches to television than simply the threefold metaphorical typology drawn up by Meyrowitz. John Corner (1997), for example, identifies four types of theory that coincide only in part with those considered by Meyrowitz. They are the theories of *representation*, affecting television's form and content especially as a vector of social 'influences' (generally considered to be negative); theories of *institution*, which single out the organizational structures of television, grounded and modelled on determined political and economic systems, as their own objective; theories of *process*, formulated in relation to processes of televisual production and consumption; and finally theories of *the medium*, the only approach where the two typologies converge.

Corner, further elaborating Meyrowitz's definition, places medium theory on a more general level than the other theoretical perspectives and acknowledges that it has a particular interest in 'the special capacity of television to transform spatial and temporal relationships and to "displace" many established forms of social experience' (Corner 1997, p. 254). The notion of flow and the conceptualization of modes of watching television, together with the corpus of studies on the 'dislocative' character of the televisual experience, are specific and recognizable emanations of medium theory. Corner commendably underlines the ready tendency of this theory to consider television *pathologically*, or at least with a certain anxiety, even if a positive attitude prevails in his followers (Corner attributes to Meyrowitz an optimism tinged with anxiety).

The considerations that I intend to develop in the present chapter pertain precisely to the perspective of medium theory, focused as has been seen on the structural characteristics that make each medium unique in its own way. I shall deal in particular with two interrelated aspects of television – the mode of supply and the mode of fruition – from a viewpoint that emphasizes possible risks while adhering to the conception of environment and to medium theory. The risks lie in yielding to the essentialism which (not only in my opinion; cf Caldwell 1995; Corner 1999) conceptualizations of the two 'modes' just cited have not been able to avoid sufficiently; and by 'essentialism' I mean the tendency, founded more on speculation than on empiricism, for the nature of the televisual medium to become fixed in a set of distinctive characters – affecting the experience of viewers – that are at the same time one-dimensional and inflexible, not merely different from but opposed to those of other media, and basically restrictive if not belittling.

When one strives to identify and isolate the specific features of a medium (or of anything else) the essentialist temptation is strong – even an expert like McLuhan did not resist it – and entirely understandable: like clear brush strokes in primary colours, the essential properties (stable, indelible, one might say monolithic) draw pictures of considerable and captivating clarity, not to mention intellectual economy, which for this reason remain easily and incisively impressed on the mind. But the results risk being the opposite of what was foreseen at the level of cognition and comprehension if (as in the case of television) it is precisely in trying to 'fix' its specificity in certain uniform and unvarying characters that we are prevented from grasping the relative individuality of its plastic and versatile nature.

2. History and critique of the flow

The figure of speech 'synecdoche' means essentially a phrase in which a part is substituted for a whole or a whole for a part, thus narrowing or widening the intended meaning. An example of the first is the poetic usage of 'sail' for 'ship'; and of the second, 'the world is cruel', referring to the cruelty of individual human beings. I recall this figure of speech because it is not unfamiliar in discourses on television; in particular, it is through a synecdoche of the second type – the whole for its parts – that television programming is conceived and connoted. I am referring to the well-known and widely used concept of the flow.

The meaning conveyed by the term 'flow' is that television programming, although it is regulated and marked out by the organized programme schedule that classifies the individual content according to its appropriateness for the various viewing times, is *not* offered to the perception and experience of viewers as a succession of distinct and separate programmes that have precise and identifiable limits. What is presented is rather a sequence of heterogeneous material, which flows forth from the screen in a continuous current: news, current affairs, talk shows, films, series and every other sort of content can be broadcast successively on the same channel within a matter of hours, mixed up with advertisements, telesales and sundry promotional material. More precisely, the phenomenon of the flow rests not so much, or not only, in the unceasing deluge and mishmash of different subject matter as in a clandestine organization and a sort of internal 'meta-coherence' (Corner 1999, p. 63) that converts parts that have no logical or thematic relationship to each other into something that can be experienced as an ongoing and (at least in part) unitary totality of programming: in short, the flow.

Among the numerous metaphors used to define television or some of its functions or *modi operandi* (window on the world, marketplace, mirror), flow is certainly the most popular and the most frequently used, both in theoretical writings and in public discourse. One may perhaps believe that a large part of this popularity is due to the word's fascination, evoking as it does the appealing image, perhaps also the sound, of fluid material running continuously and copiously, as well as its immediate syntony with a widespread idea of television as an uncontrollable and enthralling medium – and therefore an insidious one, from the point at which the flow is something to which viewers abandon themselves (perhaps gladly) and can be submerged and overwhelmed (in the matter of aquatic metaphors Todd Gitlin has gone further with his 'mediatic torrent', 2003). Anyone, writes Christopher Anderson, '...can appreciate the richness of the metaphor: it invokes the physical flow of electrons that makes television possible; the calculated flow of television content from one program or commercial to another, and a distinctive way of experiencing a broadcast medium over which a viewer may exert little control (2005, p. 2). We are almost inevitably compelled by the fascination and richness of the metaphor to portray television from the perspective of the meanings embodied in the word 'flow': meanings that in truth are none too benevolent, in their references to a current of images and sounds that are in large measure outside our control, where we can barely escape from its powerful fascination. We can share the view of John Corner (1999, p. 62) that 'flow is part of a pathology of television, a bad feature of general "programme organisation"' and that the pathologies are bound to be welcomed by its many critics among the public and the academic world. It is otherwise difficult to explain the use and abuse of a metaphor that has arisen almost as a totem of television studies and accepted as a given by nearly everyone who speaks about television.

The idea of the flow, used to conceptualize the sequential organization of televisual programme planning, was introduced for the first time over thirty years ago by the British scholar Raymond Williams, who had come fresh from the unprecedented and overwhelming experience – from the perspective of a regular viewer of British television at that time – of American commercial television. 'One night in Miami, still dazed from a week on an Atlantic liner, I began watching a film...' (Williams 1992, p. 85): is the effective and gripping start of the author's account which has now become a classic (Gripsrud 1998). In that situation Williams senses that television's offerings are composed not of a series of single programmes with well-defined and identified profiles, perhaps interrupted or spaced out by advertisements or other material, but of a pre-ordained sequence that reorders and immerses the individual scripts into a single uninterrupted flow. Thus the experience of watching television consists less of following a definite programme than of being exposed to a 'miscellaneous' succession – and to some extent a fusion – of texts, subjects, words and images: 'as if one had read two plays, three newspapers, three or four magazines, on the same day that one has been to a variety show, and a lecture and a football match. And yet in another way it is not like that at all, for though the items may be various, the televisual experience has in some important way unified them' (Williams 1992, p. 89).

The flow is a truly singular case in the history of ideas in the field of communication and the media. The idea of the flow sprang from the first 'close encounter' (White 2001) of a European intellectual, accustomed to the regular pattern of BBC programming, with the sequential – and, for an outsider, confusing – delivery of American commercial television; and was conceptualized by Williams in terms that do not dispel a suspicion of essentialism, completely alien from his intellectual habitus. Williams, in fact, attributed to the flow the significance of a defining characteristic of television, understood as much as technology as cultural form. He also affirms its central role in the field of experience – 'what seems to me the central televisual experience: the fact of the flow' (1992, p. 89) – and ends by acknowledging its status as a 'fixed property of the medium', which is precisely a way of theorizing television against which the author fulminates in the subsequent chapter of the same book (see Laing 1991, p. 167). In actual fact, the empirical evidence produced by Williams to validate the idea of the flow seems fragile and contradictory; he notices that many people generally talk about 'watching television' (another extending synecdoche) rather than watching the news or a play or a match. The evidence is also contradictory in that it is explicitly contradicted by the author, in various passages where he admits that viewers nevertheless continue to watch 'specific programmes'.

Equally striking is the fact that the notion of flow should have considerable influence, and in short that it should still survive 'as a fundamental concept in television studies' (Anderson 2005) despite having generated waves (to keep the aqueous metaphor) of criticisms and revisions over the years. John Ellis (1982) has set 'segmentation', the sub-division of contents of every type into small sequential units of picture and sound (news, commercials, transmissions of series and serials), against the concept of the flow as specific textual and televisual organization. In the wake of his studies many others (Feuer 1983; Altman 1986; Fiske 1987; Newcomb and Hirsh 1987; Laing 1991; Caldwell 1995; Ridell 1996; Gripsrud 1998) have followed up the discussion on the concept of the flow, critically redefining and reinterpreting it, sometimes exploiting the 'infinite malleability' (Laing 1991) that is one of its defects, in that the concept can be bent in the most diverse directions. Stuart Laing was already suggesting at the beginning of the 1990s that the idea of the flow should be set aside and that the most enlightening of Williams' contributions on television should be sought elsewhere. More recently John Corner expressed the hope that the 'confusing inheritance' of a notion that is now merely of historical interest was not creating further problems for television theories.

Without being in any way indifferent to the problems besetting television theory, I should prefer in this book to concentrate on the consequences of the idea of flow for the experience and enjoyment of televisual textuality, and to set out some alternatives based on a phenomenology of viewers' behaviour.

There can be no serious objection towards a notion of the flow being used, without any particular conceptual or defining claims, for the appealing and vague purpose of evoking televisual programming offered as a continuous cycle: a succession of heterogeneous material, from a number of 'sources' that vary from a few units to the hundreds of outlets in the multi-channel environment. In this connection it is possible to agree at least in part with what Jostein Gripsrud affirms: '"Flow" may survive as a name for the endless stream of sounds and images from 500 channels' (1998, p.31).

It is on the other hand very doubtful whether the flow constitutes 'the central televisual experience' for everyone or for most people, an opinion affirmed by Williams and shared explicitly or implicitly by others. The smallest pause for reflection is enough to make one realize that experiencing television as flow means being incapable of discriminating and choosing, confusing genres and programmes and being passively exposed to the deluge of an indistinct and indistinguishable miscellany of content. Such a description may apply to neophyte or 'outsider' viewers (research carried out when television first appeared indicated that viewers initially had difficulty in telling one programme apart from another; (De Rita 1964)), but not to today's expert public, or for any public that has lived with television for years. In effecting a clash between the distinctive levels of programming and the watching of television, the notion of flow proves itself to be infused with a negative and pathologizing appraisal of television-watching and of the medium itself.

We are naturally exposed to the flow in greater or lesser measure; it can even happen, when our television viewing is strictly confined to a favourite programme or one of great interest, that unless we have recorded it we do not manage to avoid watching the end of the previous programme or the start of the next one and various 'filler' items. The so-called 'pulling' strategies used by television networks aim exactly at exploiting the pulling power of flow in programming. It can equally happen that through inertia, inattention, or not least the relaxing pleasure of being freed from the effort of making a choice (cf chapter IV), we surrender more or less knowingly to the flow of images and sounds issuing from the screen.

Must we end up with a disintegration of the individuality of programmes, with the programmes becoming submerged in the flow – the parts dissolved in the acid of the whole – and ultimately dismembered by the practice of zapping? Neither the practicalities of production and marketing – the flow is fed by the creation, purchase and sale of programmes that are still individually identified by title, genre and format – nor the phenomenology of consumption (see below) can justify such a conclusion, which if anything is substantiated in the specialism of television studies. We can agree with the recent observation by McKee (2003) that the construct of television as an object to be studied seems in large measure to leave out of consideration the existence and relevance of televisual programming. A history of literature, cinema or any other art form would be inconceivable without an analysis in depth of specific writings and productions; yet a large number of stories and writings in general about television pass over programmes with scant attention and betray a substantial undervaluing of their importance. 'At the level of theory and criticism', maintained John Caughie some years ago (1990), 'it seems endemic to television writings that whereas film theory is marked by a sense of people trying to come to terms with their own almost perverse fascination – what Paul Willemen calls "cinephilia" – television theory always seems to be written by people who can see the seduction but are not seduced. The critics' fascination with the audiences in television writing may be due, at least in part, to a lack of fascination with the texts' (Caughie 1990, p. 54).

If we admit for the sake of the argument that flowing televisual programming leads us inevitably to a sequence of contents that are confusing and magmatic, then we should ask ourselves why the flow is not evoked in the entirely analogous case of sequential reading of different books. Moving on without a pause from one book to another is a frequent practice of lovers of reading, scholars and students who are preparing for an exam; this practice is not regarded as dubious, nor has the theoretical problem arisen of confusion or disintegration of the texts experienced through the continuum of reading. The solidness of the conception of the book as a unitary text, and of the reader as a subject who is capable of discernment, prevents this from happening.

In reality we, no less than readers, are capable as competent viewers of grasping 'in the twinkling of an eye' the passage from one programme to another: the replacement of a game show host by a newsreader, the switch between an American soap and an Italian one. If we were not capable of spotting even the narrow dividing lines between the various typologies of televisual content, there would be no explanation for the systematic flight from the set of the public, recorded by viewing detection systems, during commercial breaks and at the end of each programme; and the flitting between channels – driven by the search for something different – would have no sense if people were unable to tell the difference between them.

It is instructive to recall that the ability to tell the difference is a competency that is built up and refined through frequent experience of and familiarity with the things in question; the inhabitants of a foreign land all look alike to the unaccustomed gaze of the tourist, and where non-experts see only a tangle of vegetation a botanist would identify a wide variety of plants. By analogy, where absolute beginners or outsiders to television, or in all likelihood those who shun television because they despise it, will watch indiscriminately, competent viewers – that is to say, most viewers – will grasp the differences in the sequence of programmes and even of fragments, as happens when one is zapping.

But above all, the individuality and recognizability of single parts of programming-as-flow come into the open and, so to speak, get their own back every time (and it is almost impossible to find a moment in time when this does not happen) one or more specific programmes become popular, provoke discussion, become a 'must-see' (Jancovich and Lyons 2003) and create smaller or larger circles of fans and connoisseurs. 'There are certain types of programs that demand and receive focused attention' (Dayan and Katz 1992, p. 4), and, since they consist in some measure of events (cf chapter III), that impose themselves in their recognizability on viewers' memory. While television's enemies or critics generally oppose it or criticize it *en bloc*, lumping everything together and seeing the plurality of programmes as a single confused jumble, those who without being enslaved by television find it a source of interest and pleasure know well how to separate out the whole into its parts and thus make distinctions and choices. Indeed many viewers cultivate tastes and passions, develop preferences and attachments and come to have a genuine cult following (Gwenllian-Jones and Pearson 2004) for specific programmes, to which they devote their undivided and focused attention. The communities of fans gather around their favourite programmes, isolated from the flow of televisual programming.

The thoughts that I have expressed so far are not intended completely to invalidate the notion of flow, which remains applicable to a form of providing televisual content (particularly the generalist networks, it must be emphasized); nor do I wish to disregard the empirical verifiability of ways of enjoying television that have in effect been given over to programming flow. The use of television as 'wallpaper' or as a subsidiary activity (see below) is something that all of us know from direct experience or from observing the behaviour of others, and in such cases 'the diversity of programmes is less important than the permanent presence of the switched-on screen...the viewer is glued to his seat more by the uninterrupted flow of images than by the contents of the programme' (Martin Barbero 2002, p. 131–132). Not infrequently the viewer is not even in 'his or her' place, in front of the screen, but simply casts a glance or half-listens from a distance. One used to see until a few years ago, and perhaps can see today, the common sight through the open doors of the houses at street level in Naples of the television set switched on when people were not there or were taking no notice of it, engaged in some other activity in the house or street. In fact it is precisely when television becomes a simple, if important, visual and aural presence in one's life that the conditions are created for an experience that is largely emancipated from the uninterrupted flow of images: the capacity for being enthralled that forms a structural part of the flow, as much for Williams as for the strategists of televisual programming, thus becomes neutralized.

To sum up, we need to be careful not to be trapped by the synecdoche: the whole neither replaces nor nullifies the individual parts. If it is true that the supply of televisual content assumes the specific course of a flowing sequence – and it is right to identify this as an historical characteristic of the medium as we have known it up till now – it is equally true that as with books and films, television programmes possess an individuality that is discernible at both the analytical and the empirical level. The choices and practices of people's viewing are structured on this individuality, without entering into contradiction and coexisting with the structured modalities of the flow.

What I defined in the previous chapter as a 'connective approach', based on the paradigm of combination and coexistence rather than on substitution or mere alternative, is here among other things made necessary by the transformation of the distributive system, where an area of narrowcasting filled with thematic and single-subject networks has been created and expanded. If by 'flow', as originally defined by Williams, is meant not only the uninterrupted running of programmes but also the heterogeneous 'miscellany' of diverse texts and genres unified by flowing into the same sequence, then the concept is inappropriate or indeed inapplicable to the homogeneous or monovalent programming (news, or sport, or films, or documentaries) that is offered as a specialism by so many channels. Even if a documentary on the fauna of the Amazonian jungle were to be followed immediately by one on the glaciers of the South Pole, the fact that the diversity remains circumscribed within the same genre – what is more, a genre that viewers watch intentionally, from interest and enthusiasm – dispels the notion of the flow as one of television's basic constituents.

Otherwise in order to retrieve the 'miscellany' in the ambience of narrowcasting, we would have to extend or rather transfer the notion of flow from the programming sequence of each network to the ensemble of programming that is broadcast simultaneously from so many available networks. We would also have to accept that heterogeneity is made up and experienced through switching by viewers from one channel to another, which allows viewers to pass from a documentary to a film, from a reality show to a cartoon, from a talk show to a news programme, according to the speciality of the channel on which they pause for a shorter or longer time, regulated by the calm or compulsive frequency of their zapping. But not even this would be a satisfactory solution for the purpose of safeguarding the integrity of the concept, since the retrieval of the miscellany here would be at the expense of another couple of constituents of the flow: the internal meta-coherence and above all the (asserted) captivating fascination or at any rate attraction of the uninterrupted sequence for viewers, from the moment that the heterogeneous composition of texts and genres resulting from switching between networks is made possible precisely by the opposite: that is to say by the repeated interruption of the sequence by the viewer. Incidentally, we have known (if we did not already know it simply from experience) how to construct 'our' more or less heterogeneous sequences of useful content, breaking with the hidden organization and flowing continuity of the planned sequence of televisual network programming, ever since the time – we were still in a phase of broadcasting's hegemony in the 1980s – when Horace Newcomb formulated the definition and experiment of the 'viewing strip' (1999), a visual journey through prime-time programmes made up of systematic changes of channel.

From the perspective of viewers' experience, if there is doubt – as I have maintained and argued above – about the central role of the flow even in the ambit of generalist television, and in conditions of relative scarcity of supply and technological deprivation, there is all the more reason to exclude the flow from the multi-channel environment supplied by the availability of advanced technologies. The abundance of supply, which requires as never before not only the exercise of choice but also the possession of technology such as DVD, video on demand, a personal video recorder (see chapter IV in this connection) that allows one to extract programmes from the television schedule almost as if one were taking a book from the shelves of a library, create further opportunities – for those who can and wish to make use of them – to escape from the experience of televisual flow: an experience that need not be central to our viewing.

3. The glance and the gaze

I now intend to pursue the discussion from the perspective of comparing cinema with television, in order to demonstrate how the comparison between the two media has lessened in such a way as to emphasize, resolve and essentialize certain prerogatives (but no others) of the televisual medium.

Let us take the case of the spatial context of television, which provides a good example. As we all know and take for granted, television has pride of place within the walls of the home, where our private family existence is likewise located and runs its course. Although the home-specific character of the medium has in recent years begun to be questioned by studies that adduce the evidence of the wide dissemination of television screens in many public spaces, such as hotels, bars, airports, clubs and business areas – see the previous chapter (McCarthy 2001) – the much greater evidence, almost taken for granted, of the television set's localisation in the private spaces of the home, and thus the domesticity or more correctly the domesticating of the medium, is no longer a matter for discussion.

Television is firmly located within the home and the real worlds and images to which it gives access flow directly within, and blend with, the progress of everyday life: this means, in concrete terms, the dense plot of domestic activities and family relationships. Incorporated and naturalized in various domestic settings – sitting room, kitchen, children's bedrooms – the television set is *always there*, whether switched on or off or on standby: a fixture, yet not a demanding one. Television is a polysensorial medium, since it engages both sight and hearing, yet it does not necessarily have first claim on our senses. Television switched on while we are eating, while the children are playing, while we attend to personal or household tasks, *may* simply be listened to, or watched intermittently; *may* stay in the background of our visual and auditory perception and constitute what in Goffman's terms would be called a 'subsidiary involvement: an activity to which the individual can be dedicated in an absent-minded fashion, without compromising or muddling up the main task that is being done simultaneously' (Goffman 1971, p. 44).

However, there is no need to mistake conditions of possibility for conditioning that is so conclusive as to rule out any theoretical or practical alternative. Even though it has been shown to happen very frequently, the 'subsidiary' use of television does not in fact represent the only possible use, or the only use made of it. To disregard or deny this is tantamount to transforming something that is a resource, and an opportunity to integrate a substantial part of polysensorial communication with life's domestic routines, into a restrictive constraint: to regard hazy perception and intermittent attention as the principal way of using television, determined by its position in the distracting surroundings of the home.

Some overhasty theoretical conclusions concerning the 'modes' of watching television, based on and tending towards the reinforcement of an essentialist conception of the medium, have been drawn from the correct premise of its domesticated nature. Since the essentialist conceptions are as all-embracing, in their attribution of unique and definitive properties to the things being considered, as they are irreconcilable in making such properties the elements of an unshakable innate diversity between one object and another, it is not surprising that watching television should have been conceptualized in reference and contradistinction to going to the cinema. The 'glance and gaze' theories are very revealing in this connection.

It was John Ellis, in his highly influential *Visible Fiction* published at the beginning of the 1980s, who established and repeatedly asserted that 'TV's regime of vision is less intense than cinema's: it is a regime of the glance rather than the gaze. The gaze implies a concentration of the spectator's activity into that of looking; the glance implies that no extraordinary effort is being invested in the activity of looking' (1982, p. 137).

Attentive, captivated, spellbound: the gaze (of the audience) is commonly associated with film-going. Such an elective affinity takes place above all through the descent from the empirical conditions of the cinema – sitting more or less still in darkness and silence – which certainly favours visual immersion in the images of film. But it represents something more: the direct consequence of a high regard for the cultural and ethical values of the cinema. It is the density of the narrative and the magnificence, or at any rate the fascination of the cinematographic image, that incites our voyeurism and captures our gaze, keeping it spellbound by what is taking place on the screen. I note only *en passant* the nature, elitist and ethnocentric as well as being unmindful of history, of this conception of 'legitimate spectatorship'. A few decades ago, at any rate in Italy, film showings in cinemas in working-class areas would be accompanied by a lot of clamour and loud comments by the public, who shouted directly at the characters on the screen like spectators at Neapolitan melodramas. Outside the West, cinema-going in India is still characterized by intense shouting and movement on the part of spectators; people sing, talk and go in and out of the auditorium during the showing (Srinivas 2002).

The glance on the other hand – absent-minded, casual, nonchalant – is associated with television. If the theory of the gaze evokes a film buff, the theory of the glance excludes any possibility of a television buff. Once again the reason is twofold. First, the phenomenology of domestic use: 'the viewer is cast as someone who has the TV switched on, but is giving it very little attention: a casual viewer relaxing at home in the midst of the family group' (Ellis 1982, p. 162). Second, a low opinion of the aesthetics of television: unadorned, obvious, confined in most cases to showing 'talking heads', the televisual image is regarded as fundamentally incapable of attracting and captivating our gaze. Hence the importance of sound, charged with the task of prodding and reawakening the weak and fleeting attention of viewers: 'The image is the central reference in cinema. But for TV sound has a more centrally defining role... The TV image tends to be simple and straightforward, stripped of detail and excess of meanings. Sound tends to carry the details... Sound tends to anchor meaning on TV...' (Ellis 1982, p. 129).

The idea of television being watched essentially by inattentive glances from viewers who are engaged in other domestic activities but intermittently recalled by aural stimuli coming from the small screen – listeners rather than viewers, strictly speaking – has entered into our collective consciousness and created a corpus of anecdotes and case histories. How many times have we read or heard quoted the example of the housewife who follows a soap opera looking up every now and then from the ironing board? Yet there is no need to jump to facile theoretical conclusions 'just because there is an ironing board in the room' (Caldwell 1995, p. 27). As Caldwell perspicaciously observes, we have here a way of theorizing that is plainly a spin-off from (feminine) gender stereotyping, informed in turn by disparaging judgments that are reflected in the medium, its aesthetics and its field of vision. In this connection, audience research can tell us interesting things: for example, that the presence of an ironing board in the room, or at any rate the carrying out of another domestic task while watching television, is not so much the quintessence of an abstracted and casual form of consumption as a woman's way of coming to terms with the tension between her wish to abandon herself to attentive and concentrated viewing and her sense of duty towards her domestic responsibilities (at times greater than their importance and urgency might justify). 'Many of the women feel that to just watch television without doing anything else at the same time would be an indefensible waste of time, given their sense of their domestic obligations' (Morley 1986, p. 150; but see also Gauntlett and Hill 1999). On the other hand, a mode of lateral viewing can equally prove to be a source of gratification and emotional involvement; the fact that soap operas, for example, or other daytime programmes must often share the attention of female viewers with the ironing board does not stop the viewers from experiencing a deep sense of participation in, and a great deal of pleasure from, the events taking place on the screen.

We have no right to jump to conclusions, even if there is a silent telephone in the room or in the house: the telephone which (according to an anecdote that is the more whispered and confidential because it is infused with a vague sense of shame, or indeed guilt) other viewers of both sexes 'confess' to unplugging so as not to be disturbed while they are watching their favourite programmes, soap operas or anything else. We like to immerse ourselves in this kind of viewing with undivided attention, our eyes glued to the screen. The derisive epithet 'couch potatoes' would not have become so widespread if the image, even if it is exaggerated, of viewers sprawling on the sofa and almost incapable of taking their eyes off the television set did not have a certain credibility. In fact the entire edifice of accusations against the powerful effects of the medium would be doomed to collapse if the way of watching television were reduced to cursory glances that, it is presumed, would be incapable of sustaining an influential relationship; just as the possibility, if not the general practice, of engaging in another activity while watching television should at least prompt some reflection on the contradiction between this hyperactive multi-tasking and the inertia generally ascribed to those who watch television.

In reality we have here the baseless conflict between diverse ways of appropriating objects and cultural material, of which only one – the cinematographic mode, or the literary mode according to Abercrombie (1996, p. 182) – is considered legitimate, since it functions as the touchstone in relation to the others. Different conceptions and ways of using time are equally implicated in this conflict, which brings us back to the distinction, neither oppositional nor hierarchical, between 'monochronic time' and polychronic time' that has been formulated by Edward Hall (1984, pp. 44–58): the regime of the first means 'doing one thing at a time'; the second, 'doing many things at once'. So just as television creates the conditions of 'polygamy of place' (cf chapter I), it also (like radio) makes 'polychrony of time' accessible on the level of the chronemic experience.

Between the perspective of the ironing board (theory of the glance) and that of the unplugged telephone or the all-enveloping sofa – which takes us back to the theory of the gaze, even if in a degraded sense of supine and passive dependency rather than intense and ecstatic fascination – *there is therefore no conflict.* As personal experience and the observation of others are well placed to demonstrate, if we can only have faith in them, the ways of watching television include *both the glance and the gaze.* Both are appropriate, according to the circumstances and our inclinations and both are made possible by the domestic nature of the context. However inelegant the formulation may seem, we must agree with James Lull when he affirms that 'different types of programs elicit different styles of viewing for different people at different moments of the day' (1990, p. 166).

In the ambience of the home, interwoven with relationships and duties, it can happen at some times of day and stages of life more than others that a switched-on television set provides a counterpoint or background to our main occupations or, if we are lonely, gives us the company of human voices and pictures that require no more than a glance from time to time, just to confirm that they are there.

But the home is also a privileged place where we can 'pull the plug' on intellectual and practical tasks and give ourselves over to the pleasure of a short or longer rest. In these moments – for example, on getting home from work, or in the intervals between one task and another, or at the end of the day – watching television primarily fulfils the need to relax. We tend to pay only passing attention, in a relaxed fashion, to what is taking place on the small screen, with a glance that is perhaps not fully concentrated but well inclined to remain turned towards the source, or the instrument, of our relaxed state of mind. We have to admit that this sort of enjoyment is not infrequently to be found in the cinema, demanding a shorter and less intensive attention span than the voyeuristic and impassioned immersion in the world of film.

Although the theory of the glance may deny it, in clear contradiction to speculations on television's hypnotic power, television can be not only a background and a means to lateral involvement, but also a primary focus of interest, attention and gaze. Here the gap, which refers back to the factors discussed in the previous paragraph, lies between generic and non-selective 'television watching' and the viewing of specific programmes, chosen in accordance with preferences, tastes and pleasures with which we can sympathize. Audience research, regular features in popular newspapers and Internet sites, fan clubs, everyday conversation and personal experience all demonstrate without a shadow of doubt the existence and spread of a form of highly committed and motivated television-watching by enthusiastic viewers who are very knowledgeable about this or that programme down to the smallest detail. These programmes are watched with rapt attention, sometimes in company (when the predilection is shared by others), sometimes in the solitude that is made possible by having several sets in different parts of the home and whose purpose is to eliminate any kind of interruption; they are watched with a gaze that is every bit as intense and dedicated as in the cinema. More often than is believed, the televisual image is able to reward this rapt attention on the level of aesthetic pleasure: many television programmes of all types pursue the stylistic and formal distinction and tempt their viewers' appetites with a rich and refined 'televisuality', to quote John Caldwell's definition (1995).

But even in its poorest programmes, when the show consists of nothing but talking heads, the televisual image can seem very attractive. It offers up the faces and bodies of political and television personalities, protagonists in stories and events, ordinary people to the curious, empathetic or ruthless gaze of its viewers: faces and bodies that are full of symbolic indications to be read or scrutinized. We see tears welling up and flowing, we perceive unchecked reactions, we guess that someone has had a facelift, sometimes we move closer to the screen to have a better look at a detail, if for no other reason than to experience the pleasure of staring unseen at a stranger without having to feel embarrassed by our impertinence.

Television effectively allows us to indulge in behaviour that is different from that which is generally regarded as being 'appropriate' in other circumstances of our social and cultural life, since we can be more flexible and less inhibited by prescriptive constraints. Going to the cinema or the theatre or visiting a museum are activities that are normally not easily combined with the possibility (and above all with the acceptability) of doing something else simultaneously. We may not chatter during a film or a play or in a library, nor raise our voices during a visit to a museum; and although there is a margin of tolerance of such behaviour everywhere (in practice everything is done in the cinema, from munching food to kissing and cuddling) we, or those who may ask us to behave more appropriately, are aware that we have broken a rule that allows concentrated and committed enjoyment. This rule in turn is relevant not only to the actual conditions pertaining to participation, which in the cited examples happens in public venues and in presence of strangers who have every right not to be annoyed, but also to the symbolic status of those cultural experiences considered to be 'elevated', such as the cinema, reading or theatre: things of this type demand the respect of dedicated and absorbed behaviour.

These situational norms and prescriptions can, however, be evaded in the specific circumstances of television in the home. This possibility manifests itself particularly when television lets us watch ceremonial events of all types (religious, civil, artistic and social) at home. Here it is not so much, or not only, the question of the glance or the gaze that is the point at issue as the modality of participation in public events within the domestic space (see the next chapter). If every situation is at the same time prescriptive and proscriptive (Meyrowitz 1993), in the sense that it demands certain types of behaviour and prohibits others – the examples quoted above concerning the cinema and the library are valid here – then ceremonial and ritual events demand still stricter adherence to correct behaviour. You would not be admitted in jeans and a T-shirt to an opening night at La Scala, where black tie is obligatory; and if you attend a religious ceremony you are obliged to behave respectfully and formally, even if you do not join in the singing and the prayers.

But it is a fact that the prescriptive and proscriptive demands of ceremonial occasions and public events take a back seat when participation takes place through the means of television in the ambience of the home. Once we are no longer in the direct presence of the event and the social control and power exercised by the other spectators – two factors that determine our respect for the rules – a wide range of behaviour patterns is open to us, from the most conventional to the most disrespectful, essentially at the viewers' discretion. It is not by chance that the first televised transmissions of important civil and religious ceremonies aroused anxiety, in certain countries, on the part of the authorities that they would be watched in an inappropriate and disrespectful manner by viewers who were safely protected from the eyes of authority (Scannell 1996). A flippant attitude towards ceremonies on television is indeed a possibility, just as the opposite is possible: that is to say, engaged participation in and concentration on the ceremony, not unlike the behaviour required and expected at the live event. Some of the faithful probably follow the Mass on television as if they were in church (while others continue to lay the table during a Papal benediction) and the anecdote, possibly invented but much quoted, of the teenager in tears because she had nothing to wear for the televised wedding of Charles and Diana is just one example of many. This example, it is worth emphasizing, is to be adduced as evidence *not* of television's disorientating influence on the perception of the boundary between direct and mediatized experience, but of the possibility that television sometimes offers – to viewers who are disposed to become involved, if we naively agree to take the example cited at face value – the opportunity to go beyond the domestic context and to participate in distant events with undivided attention and the feeling of being 'actually there' – yet without the obligation to observe the rules of public behaviour that are imposed in specific situations.

In the home environment which by its very nature is imbued with mostly routine practices and experiences, the televisual experience coexists with the various tasks and commitments of domestic life and the continual shifting of our attention span: sometimes focused on the ensemble of pictures and sounds emanating from the screen, sometimes distracted by tasks and demands that relegate the switched-on set to the background.

But it is precisely because television allows us to switch between looking and listening, between involvement and detachment, and because it offers us both demanding and relaxing forms of cultural entertainment and social participation, that it can claim to possess the true and authentically distinctive qualities of an open medium. It is flexible; and it is resistant both to theoretical imposition and to the empirical experience of fixed, essential and unchanging characteristics.

3

TELEVISION CEREMONIES
THE DOUBLE CORONATION OF MOTHER TERESA OF CALCUTTA

1. The theory of media events

Mother Teresa's beatification ceremony took place in St Peter's Square on Sunday 19 October 2003 in the presence of hundreds of thousands of pilgrims who had flocked to the Vatican from all parts of the world. At the same time a vast public, consisting of millions of individuals scattered throughout the globe, was able to follow the same ceremony on their television sets in the home or on giant screens out of doors, filmed and broadcast live by 77 television networks in 40 countries. In Italy over 40 per cent of viewers tuned in to this liturgical celebration: in terms of audience share, it was the religious programme watched by the largest number of people in 2003.

That same evening the first part of the biographical miniseries *Mother Teresa* went out on the Italian television channel Raiuno. It was watched by nearly 10 million viewers (this number was to rise to 11 million the following evening, making *Mother Teresa* the most popular television drama of the 2003–2004 season. The broadcasting of the miniseries at the same time as the beatification ceremony was carefully planned and repeatedly announced. Some observers deplored what seemed to them to be a cynically irreverent use of a sacred rite (the beatification ceremony) as a 'trailer' for a secular piece of entertainment (the television drama). There are in truth good grounds for claiming that on 19 October 2003 a real ceremony and a fiction programme, each aimed at celebrating Mother Teresa in its own way, were connected in order to produce a unique, indeed *sui generis*, media event. In this chapter I shall use the case study of an unprecedented co-operation between a (relatively rare and in any case special) religious ritual and a secular drama – both with great audience appeal, both conveyed through the means of television – as an opportunity to introduce, discuss and perhaps supplement the theory of media events.

The concept of the media event or televisual ceremony has been developed and systematized with great analytical precision by Daniel Dayan and Elihu Katz in a book published in 1992, which soon became a classic of mediological literature.

The authors start from a number of assumptions that we have met and thematized in the two previous chapters – despatialized simultaneity, the regime of the gaze, although they do not adopt this exact conceptual vocabulary – in order to arrive at the identification of a typology of programmes which, by virtue of their special nature, demand and receive focused attention and intense involvement from the largest possible national and international audiences. We are concerned with events in the proper sense, not infrequently ones of historic importance (the sub-title of the English edition of the book is 'The live broadcasting of history'): events which although they have an existence of their own, separate from television, in the sense that they would have taken place anyway, become very much more important and valuable in the field of individual and collective human experience, thanks to the fact that television shoots them and broadcasts them to the remotest corners of the country, or indeed of the whole planet. The televisual medium by its inherent capacity makes possible a temporal co-presence that breaks the chains of spatial distance and gives individuals access to shared experiences that would otherwise be impossible for them to enjoy or even to imagine. This capacity comes into play and is enhanced as never before in the case of media events, which create the conditions of simultaneous televisual exposure and viewing on a vast scale, whether from the perspective of the number of viewers, the range of localities reached or the geographical distances covered. What we see at work in similar cases is the maximum expression of broadcasting's technological potential. As the authors themselves emphasize, in keeping with the principle and capacity of the technology, television (and radio) would be perfectly capable at any time of reaching anyone, anywhere, directly and simultaneously. It does not happen that way, owing to a series of institutional, social, cultural, technical and economic factors that get in the way; but these and other barriers are surmounted on the occasion of televisual events.

Furthermore, and more important than its technological potential, it is the integrating function of television that is expressed with greater intensity on the occasion of media events. In declaring that such events originate and emanate from the 'centre' of society – television narrates them, but does not create them – Dayan and Katz put the emphasis on the strength of social integration, which is closely connected with situations where multitudes of isolated individuals, scattered communities and people of a diaspora find themselves sharing the extraordinary experience of being present at events that are at the heart of national or international society and thus express and celebrate a nucleus of common values. Such values, the authors specify, are consensual and reconciling, so that their universal appeal attracts and keeps together a disunited and distant public through television, if only for the limited duration (a few hours or a few days) of the event.

The theory of media events was developed under the strong influence of social anthropology, especially Victor Turner's works on the symbolic order, and clearly derives part of his own conceptual reasoning from this source. The theory affirms the eminently ceremonial nature of this special genre of programmes (not by chance, the French edition that was published four years after the English one was titled *La télévision cérémonielle*, 1996.) We are concerned not solely with the fact that many of the events being analysed are *per se* civil or religious ceremonies (weddings, funerals, coronations), but with the ensemble of conditions that create, according to the authors' definition, 'festive television' and a 'festive viewing' of television: that is to say, a break in daily activities, a disruption of normal programming and viewing, to make room not for an unexpected irruption – like the fatal accident in the Alma tunnel in Paris – but for the exceptional occurrence of an event that is planned and expected, such as the funeral of Princess Diana in London. Ceremonial or festive television is the result of complex negotiations between three main categories of social participants: the organizations in charge of organizing the event, the broadcasters who film it and transmit it, and the public themselves who corroborate the importance of the event by making themselves available to watch it, not infrequently through prior planning (cancelling other engagements, arranging group viewing). In this connection, the authors and especially Dayan (1997a) do not hesitate to speak of a 'contract' which sanctions the character of media events as a democratic ritual.

This agreement between the parties constitutes the event as a televisual ceremony: a new metamorphic species of the ceremonial situation. The way in which the traditional conception and experience of the ceremony is reconverted into a televisual ceremony is twofold and interrelated: the simultaneous presence of all participants in the same place, which for the greater part of collective ceremonies has a palpable dimension of physicality (the contact with people's bodies in the crowd, for example), has disappeared; while the usually public nature of the event is combined with the private nature of the home environment where the ceremony will be enjoyed.

One may ask whether a public ceremony suffers a certain devaluing or degradation of its component parts – the ceremonial dimension and the public dimension – in consequence of being linked with the domestic space. This question is as relevant as it is insidious. We can easily be persuaded to agree with the argument concerning publicity and loss of ceremony, while falling into the temptation to judge the new by old-fashioned or inappropriate standards. Clearly this is not the case with the theory of media events: one of the main aims of that theory is to lend transparency and value to the 'retextualization' of the ceremonial, and to the redrawing of the symbolic boundaries between public and private space which – quite unlike a simple privatization of what is public – takes place in the home viewing of collective events. As we have seen in the previous chapter, the domestic ambience is liable to loosen or dissolve the prescriptive and proscriptive constraints of behaviour that befits a ceremonial occasion. Nevertheless an event that someone watches at home 'eating an apple' – as Dayan (1997b), referring to a statement by the philosopher Alain Finkielkraut, has emphasized – does not for this reason cease to be a ceremony, followed and participated in by others, and often in groups (of family, friends or neighbours) who reproduce on the domestic scale the collective dimension of the event and give life to the micro-forums where a public opinion can be developed and expressed.

Although the author (Rajagopal 2001) does not present it in the interpretative framework of a media event, I think that one of the most vivid and eloquent examples of ceremonial participation and the reconfiguration of domestic into public space has been offered by the case of *Ramayan*. This epic-religious serial enjoyed astonishing and phenomenal popularity in India at the beginning of the 1980s. Rajagopal makes a profound and well-documented analysis of it as part of a much-quoted study of the relationship between television and the transformation of the Indian political scene (I declare now that in citing a serial as an example of a televisual ceremony I am deviating from the strict orthodoxy surrounding the concept of media events). Rajagopal refers to viewers who completed their ritual ablutions before the serial started, decorated the television set with flowers and surrounded it with burning joss sticks; he also testifies from personal experience to the hospitality that anyone could count on, even in the home of strangers, if they were in the street or else far from their own home when *Ramayan* was being transmitted; they would knock on the door of the nearest house and be welcomed in a natural way: 'There was a mutual acknowledgement of the occasion, and a wordless readiness to share it, although we were otherwise unrelated' (page 94).

To go back to the sources: Dayan and Katz identify three main categories of media events, which they define respectively as Competitions, Conquests and Coronations. Competitions have pride of place in sport and politics; Conquests (generally less frequent) equate to the great leaps forward for mankind, for example, in the field of science; and Coronations are solemn forms of 'glorification', celebrations of the rites of passage of 'heroes': weddings, funerals, assumptions of the highest offices such as genuine coronations and (although the authors do not mention these other-worldly rites of passage that belong to Catholic tradition) beatifications and canonizations.

So media events or televisual ceremonies – subject to certain conditions, of which an essential one is 'liveness' or filming on the spot, a point that I shall return to later – can include a royal wedding or a coronation, a Papal journey, the Olympic Games, the moon landing, the signing of a peace treaty, the funeral of someone of global importance, the Oscar ceremonies, the final match of a world championship...and so on: events that have been planned for a long time and pre-announced, which television does not produce or organize but broadcasts to the remotest places, thus allowing very large audiences, both national and international, to attend simultaneously. It thus fulfils, through the coming together of so many micro-communities geographically dispersed in a huge despatialized community, the conditions enabling the cultural integration on a large scale that is among the most important functions of ceremonial television, as the greatest expression of broadcasting's potential.

The theory of media events has not failed to arouse controversy. Nick Couldry (2003) has made a meticulous critique of the neo-Durkheimian type of functionalism that shapes crucial assumptions, especially the assertion that shared values emanating from the 'core' of society find elements in televisual events that have, so to speak, a 'coagulating' effect, in that they keep the diverse and disunited parts of society together. James Carey (1998) for his part has argued strongly against the idea of ceremonial television being inspired by consensual values, demonstrating through convincing case studies the existence of televisual ceremonies that have their roots in the stony ground of dissent and social conflict. Others have commented that the types of event considered by the authors already belong in all probability to a televisual world that is gone for good (Scannell 1995).

Whether or not such criticisms are, or appear to be, justified, it should be recognized that the theory of media events is measured against some of the most crucial questions connected with the changes introduced by television in the public and private life of modern society; it also looks at these questions from unconventional viewpoints. Thus, for example, whereas a large proportion of television studies are concerned with the everyday and daily dimension of the medium, the continuous flow of programming and the casual and inattentive viewer, Dayan and Katz draw attention to and elaborate on the interruption of the daily routine, the suspension of the flow, the festive dimension of television, and redeem the supposed passivity of the viewer, assuming a public that performs well, participates and is prepared to be mobilized. Equally, attending a ceremonial event in the home is not pathologized as an indication, or an aggravation, of the emptying of the public sphere drained by an inevitable privatization, but acknowledged as an unprecedented opportunity for those (most people) who cannot be 'on the spot' to be present at a distance. The peculiarly sociological preoccupation with the constitution of the community and the maintenance of social links reigns supreme. Where the conditions do not exist for establishing a community that is visible, localized and physically in contact, televisual ceremonies offer the opportunity for invisible meetings with scattered multitudes, temporarily brought together as a large imagined community (Benedict Anderson's work is certainly in the minds of the authors of *Media Events*). As Dayan has said (1997b), 'there is no good reason to disqualify [certain events]' just because they are exceptional or involve ephemeral communities that last only for the duration of the event and sometimes not even that. They remind us that the social and televisual world that we have lost, or are losing, can be found again and can acquire a new lease of life through the ceremonial and festive highlights of the most ordinary and domestic among the media.

2. The global celebrity of a 'living saint'

Religious ceremonies such as beatification and canonization do not necessarily or automatically emerge as media events, despite their relative rarity (during the pontificate of John Paul II they followed one another with unaccustomed frequency) and despite the attention that television, in a Catholic country like Italy, does not fail to give to Church rituals, in particular to festive celebrations in St Peter's Square. The 'event-like' character of Mother Teresa's beatification should therefore be reconstructed and justified by starting above all with the figure of the person being beatified: without doubt one of the most popular personalities of the second half of the twentieth century, an emblem of the charitable ardour to be found in other times, and yet a heroine of our times by virtue of being a top celebrity on the global media scene.

One remarkable manifestation must be numbered among the numerous civil and religious initiatives in Calcutta celebrating the beatification of Mother Teresa, barely six years after her death: a festival of films and documentaries dedicated to her (the *Mother Teresa Film Festival*). Although one can find films, at any rate in the history of Italian cinema and television (for example, those on Francis of Assisi, Maria Goretti and Don Bosco), and especially television serials dedicated to one saint or another and sometimes to more than one (two miniseries on Padre Pio, the same number on John XXIII, three on John Paul II, the film and the television series on Maria Goretti), in none of these cases would there have been enough filmographical material for a festival centred on a single religious figure. What makes this circumstance still more unusual is the fact that a fair number of the titles in the festival were produced while the 'saint of the gutters', as Mother Teresa was described on account of her tireless devotion to helping the derelict and dying to escape from their miserable fate on urban pavements and dusty shanty towns, was still alive.

The series of films about Mother Teresa began in 1969 with the BBC documentary *Something Beautiful for God*, which was a decisive factor in acquainting the western world with the personality and work of the founder of 'Missionaries of Charity'. It was furthermore the occasion of a highly resonant conversion of the producer, the formerly cynical and agnostic English polemicist Malcolm Muggeridge. Next came *Mother Teresa, Her Legacy*, by the Canadian nun Ann Petrie, which won two Emmy awards; *Mother Teresa and Her World*, a Japanese production; *Total Surrender*, produced by the American Catholic Eternal World Television Network; and *In the Name of God's Poor*, by the French author Dominique Lapierre. The list contains at least ten more titles in addition to those mentioned, but we should add *Hell's Angel*; this one was made for Channel 4 in 1994 by the journalist Christopher Hitchens, a relentless critic of Mother Teresa and author of a book *The Missionary Position* that attracted heated controversy. Mother Teresa's mission has also inspired a musical, a ballet by Maurice Béjart and a cartoon series.

Even those who are unaware of the existence of this corpus of media products probably know about the significant role played by the media in transforming Mother Teresa – an exceptional person by virtue of the indomitable energy and determination which she devoted to caring for the world's outcasts – into a global celebrity. Millions of people all over the world have become familiar with her small bent form, her furrowed face, her white habit trimmed with missionary blue, having seen her repeatedly on their television screens and in the pages of newspapers and glossy magazines: receiving the Nobel Peace Prize in 1979, her frequent audiences with the Pope, her hand being held by Princess Diana, being received respectfully by world leaders, in moments of prayer, leaning over babies, the sick, the dying, all of them welcomed into her hospices that were open to those who everyone had abandoned.

If it seems disrespectful to define her as a 'media celebrity' – many celebrities or media stars fall into the category of people who are merely 'known for being known', which certainly does not apply to Mother Teresa – one can nevertheless affirm that the 'living saint' became a 'media friend' (Meyrowitz 1993), for those, at any rate in part, who repeatedly came across her in television and the press: a familiar figure, almost like a friend. Seen in this way, the case of Mother Teresa seems at the same time a common one, yet unique; a case that is symptomatic of our times and yet exceptional.

It is a characteristic of today's mediatized and globalized society that the media are the creators and multipliers – on a local and, more significantly, a worldwide scale – of the celebrity of individuals who are in one way or another out of the ordinary, or *extra-ordinary* in the sense that they fall outside the category of ordinariness. This can be said of Mother Teresa. Equally typical of present-day experience is our familiarization with media celebrities, which not infrequently generates unilateral affection and a feeling of friendship; this arises from the inextricable relationship between notoriety and presence on the media scene, that is to say in front of our eyes and in the ambience of our lives. Taking another global celebrity as an example, Antony Giddens has noted in this connection that 'when the image of Nelson Mandela may be more familiar to us than the face of our next-door neighbour, something has changed in the nature of our everyday experience' (1999, pp. 11–12).

It is perhaps not unrelated to what I have said above that Mother Teresa, particularly when she was still alive, should according to research carried out in various countries have ended up as one of the most admired personalities of the present day, in the mixed company of pop idols, sport champions and the 'evergreen' Che Guevara.

But the unique and exceptional character of the mediatic resonance that accompanied the impressive project and figure of the Nun of Calcutta, and made her 'more familiar than our next-door neighbour' to many people in all parts of the world, rests in her 'saintliness'. Like Padre Pio da Pietralcina (who however lived in the pre-television era and was the object of a cult that was expressed and nourished by direct or close contact with the faithful, in pilgrimages, and in participation in religious rituals celebrated by the friar), Mother Teresa did not have to await the canonization process to be considered a saint. She was 'a living saint'. But in making her into a global celebrity the media triggered off an unprecedented process of familiarization with which is considered by many people, not necessarily from an entirely sceptical and disenchanted perspective, to be somewhat outmoded by present-day standards, or else redolent of the naive religious beliefs of earlier times: the actual concept of sainthood and its incarnation in human beings.

Furthermore, the nun of Calcutta, in her deep immersion in the most tragic realities of today's world recalls in some respects the exemplary figures of earlier times (or those whom our limited confidence in the present induces us to relegate to the past): we need only think of her life being totally devoted to an altruistic project, her fervour in caring for bodies devastated by Aids and leprosy, and in kissing the lepers and treating infected wounds without shrinking from physical contact. Stories of this kind have been handed down to us through the lives of medieval saints as recognizable signs of sainthood. But if we leave a territory which demands great tact by virtue of being a matter of faith, the fact remains that the media have helped to make Mother Teresa into one of the most beloved and respected personalities of the second half of the twentieth century: a celebrity and even a global legend, cutting across people of every generation, class, ethnicity, nationality and creed. If they have succeeded in this enterprise, it is because the personality and work of Mother Teresa were clearly capable of representing an ideal endowed with universal sensibility, if not a model to be universally imitated – even though, inspired as she was by values such as self-sacrifice, generosity and poverty that are apparently alien to a modern world imbued with egoism and materialism, she was not spared damaging criticisms of her deep aversion to birth control, her exaltation of the 'grace' of physical suffering and her refusal to take a stance against the political causes of destitution and those responsible for deserting the poor. And certainly Mother Teresa's goal, followed up and put into practice, that the dying should have the comfort of human presence and contact, must have struck a deep chord in universal sensibility, unhappily aware of the present-day 'loneliness of the dying' (Elias 1991).

One might find it somewhat of a paradox that this demanding ideal, marked by total self-renunciation in favour of others, has proved to be not entirely incompatible with a goal to which many millions aspire: success, more especially if it is built up and sanctified by the media. Mother Teresa was without any doubt a successful person (if not exactly 'the most powerful woman of the twentieth century', if we go by the hyperbolic definitions thought up by journalists): she carried out almost impossible charitable works, mobilized thousands of missionaries and volunteers, attracted impressive flows of donations, was awarded the Nobel Peace Prize and a string of other prestigious international awards, received a tribute from the UN, had access to world leaders, was on familiar terms with the Pope – all this constituted and displayed unequivocal signs of the huge success of her altruistic enterprise.

From this perspective Mother Teresa, devoted to the poorest of the poor like a medieval saint and in the name of an ethos supposedly of another era, represented a figure entirely in harmony with the exploitation of success: success that is accompanied and reinforced by visibility on the contemporary world media scene. She has furthermore offered an unprecedented and perhaps unrepeatable example of the path taken by altruism (or, for the faithful, by holiness) to global celebrity.

3. Two coronations

Like Princess Diana – whose wedding and funeral were both grand televisual events – Mother Teresa had the rare privilege of being the protagonist in two 'coronations': first her funeral and then her beatification. Perhaps because it struck a world community that was already worn out by the recent demonstrations of grief occasioned by the tragic and premature death of Princess Diana, the death of Mother Teresa at the age of nearly 90 at the beginning of September 1997 seemed to arouse relatively less emotional reaction and perhaps a smaller amount of spectatorial participation at her funeral. The state funeral decreed by the Indian government nevertheless provided an authentic televisual event, which was given this form by being broadcast live on public and private networks in over thirty countries. An audience estimated at some hundreds of millions watched the ceremony in their own homes or followed it on giant screens erected in public spaces. In Italy, where the live transmission of the funeral began at around 5 a.m. on 13 September 1997, it reached a level of 47 per cent of audience share and, in general, notched up a record as the longest broadcast of a public event on Mondovisione.

In conferring worldwide visibility on the inter-faith and inter-class nature of a ceremony attended by participants from the widest possible range of religious beliefs and by government representatives from a large number of countries, alongside the crowd of poor and simple people, television enhanced and brought to the general public 'the shift from an "indicative" definition of reality (reality as what is) to a "subjunctive" one (reality as what could or should be)' (Dayan and Katz 1992, 104). This shift is a prerogative of grand ceremonial events that are inspired by consensual and universalistic values.

We may similarly speak of Mother Teresa's beatification ceremony, which I have already mentioned at the beginning of this chapter, as a televisual event with very similar characteristics to her funeral. In this instance, however, we are faced with a metamorphosis of the event, sparked off by the co-operation between two television genres that were different from each other yet came together for the purposes of the occasion: the live morning transmission of the beatification ceremony and the evening broadcast of the miniseries, both of them dedicated to the celebration of Mother Teresa and 'irradiating' the religious and human values associated with her person and her work.

The new type of event, re-textualized or rather 're-genred' in so far as it is constituted in the sequence and cross-reference between two genres (fact and fiction) undergoes a diminishing of scale in the metamorphosis: from international to national, since the opportunity to watch the 'first night' of the miniseries was clearly given only to the Italian viewing public. But the fact that only they had this experience does not lessen the unprecedented singularity of the componential and hybrid televisual celebration that was orchestrated around Mother Teresa's beatification. We must now outline the role of television drama in the setting-up of the event, in the wider context of Italian televisual narrative of the religious genre.

4. The Catholic imagination

I have shown above how the biographical miniseries devoted to Mother Teresa of Calcutta was the most watched television drama in the 2003–2004 season, attracting an average audience of over 10 million viewers for the two instalments. Viewing figures of this order of magnitude are becoming rarer, in a televisual environment where the audiences of most generalist networks are starting to complain about the erosion and dispersal of the multi-channel system; but these audiences still in large measure watch religious dramas.

From the year 2000, the Jubilee Year, the most successful television dramas in every season were in Italy almost automatically associated with tales of the 'exemplary life' of an important religious personality who was an object of mass worship and of the canonization process: the two *Padre Pio* dramas (1999–2000 and 2000–2001); *Papa Giovanni* (Pope John XXIII: 2001–2002); *Madre Teresa* (2003–2004); *Karol* (Pope John Paul II: 2004–2005). But the religious narrative dramas that reached the highest levels of popularity in the first seasons of the new millennium did not constitute an exceptional or unexpected manifestation of the close link between the supply and the consumption of the Italian religious stories: a link that is predicated upon the strong and lasting nature of Catholic sentiment. Stories that in one way or another draw on the religious inspiration of the national collective imagination have for years catered for a trend that not only encouraged the increased production of home-grown television drama, but also – at any rate up till now and with insignificant exceptions – had a guaranteed appeal to a vast public. In a market of cultural goods such as television, characterized by a structural uncertainty where despite expectations many programmes are unsure of audience results, religious drama in Italy provide the largest possible guarantee of a popular success.

As well as the examples cited above, the twelve titles of the Bible Project (from *Abraham* to the *Revelation of St John the Divine*) testify to this; likewise the proliferation of biographies of the last two Popes, the lives of saints (*Maria Goretti, St Francis, St Anthony of Padua, Rita of Cascia*) and the stories of appearances by the Virgin Mary (*Lourdes, Fatima*). These are all programmes whose audience ratings are more than satisfactory and sometimes remarkable.

Such an accumulation of narrative supply, correlated with the religious sentiments of the Italian public and repaid by that public with a generous and apparently inexhaustible enjoyment of the programmes, depicts an Italian scene that, at any rate in this particular respect, can be considered unique in the world. Foreign observers happen to be surprised about this, their surprise perhaps reflecting the sympathetic but culturally relativist attitude of someone who is noticing some strange instance of folklore. On the other hand it is not unusual to detect even in Italian observers and critics an attitude of barely concealed condescension towards a typology of programmes that are attuned to religious sentiment, which is supposed to pertain to the more traditional and less secularized elements of the country.

There is no doubt that the secularization process in present-day Italy is less advanced and more unevenly distributed in society than in other countries. In fact the peculiar nature of the 'case of Italy' does lends itself to explanations or explicative hypotheses concerning the frequent supply and widespread popularity of religious dramas. Nevertheless this cannot simply be ascribed to cultural backwardness.

As the sociologist of religion Franco Garelli (2003) has amply and persuasively pointed out in recent times, Italy is distinguished from other Catholic countries in the field of religion by the persistence of a strong and majority-held sense of belonging to the Catholic faith, seen and perceived by most Italians as a fundamental part of their collective identity as well as of their national history. This widespread feeling is relatively independent from the practice of religious ritual, observed these days only by a minority (if a substantial one) of the population; it is even independent of the observance of the sexual and family morals preached by the Church. If anything, it is precisely the pluralist way of interpreting and showing forth religious sentiments – a recurring trait of Catholic Italy and not a new one – and the high level of tolerance on the part of the Church in the face of such diversification that creates and maintains the conditions for lasting adherence to the Catholic faith. This adherence persists not in opposition to or in spite of, but within and through, the processes of secularization and modernization – to which, incidentally, the Catholic religion is not (within limits) opposed or hostile.

The strength of Italian Catholicism in present-day society owes much, adds Garelli, to what he calls 'the affective approach to the truth': a strategy aimed at recovering and maintaining ecclesiastical authority based not so much on doctrinaire and prescriptive admonitions as on the communicative effectiveness of a religious message: a message that proves its truth in the context of charitable deeds and in a commitment to the most important matters of civil coexistence that offers constant reference points on the profound meaning of life. All this takes place in a land that is enriched more than any other by historical religious memories whose visible traces are scattered throughout the land, in numberless places of worship, art galleries, in towns and villages and in literature. A 'Catholic imagination' comes to life from this, populated by saints, statues, churches, cathedrals, stained glass windows, paintings and Nativity scenes; this allows symbols, icons and religious points of reference to be deeply rooted in Italians' collective imaginary, and is in all probability related to their lasting Catholic sentiment, even if they are in large measure unaware of it.

This is enough to help us better to understand the phenomenon, neither eccentrically 'folklorist' nor attributable to the tenacity of tradition, of the success of religious television drama in Italy. We should perhaps also note the escalation of a success of this kind, which has paralleled an equally intensified demand since the beginning of the new millennium. Religious figures who are loved and surrounded by immense popular devotion, like John XXIII and Padre Pio, the divine figure of Christ, a benevolent and universally admired and respected person like Mother Teresa, a holy child symbolizing purity like Maria Goretti: protagonists of such standing, whose earthly presence lives on and resonates in our memories after their death, are obviously the creators and prime movers of the success enjoyed by the productions that are dedicated to them. But the difference in comparison with other stories is one of degree, not substance: religious dramas broadcast in the first years of the new millennium, whatever their characters and plot, have always attracted audiences of considerable size.

Perhaps we should mention the *Zeitgeist* that permeates the start of the third millennium and, by adding the destabilizing and worrying impact of the outbreak of serious conflicts in the world to the bewilderment connected to the changes of the millennium, has a considerable impact on the individual and collective awareness of the current human condition and its destiny. Even though we may not sense all this in the ordinary and largely unreflective course of our daily life, we are enveloped if not infused with an atmosphere of insecurity and danger and face much foggy uncertainty, both material and symbolic, in the future.

There have never been more appropriate circumstances for what we might identify as a need and a demand for points of reference, solid anchorage-points and ethical compass-bearings – if indeed to define this as a need for the sacred and transcendent would lead us too quickly to abstract and facile conclusions. These would be still more convincing if they were incarnated in and 'communicated' by charismatic figures, whose authority and exemplary nature was acknowledged by popular sentiment. We should not therefore be surprised if television drama in precisely these circumstances has more recourse than ever – and the public allows itself to be led *en masse* – to the rich store of sense and the massive heritage of salvific and charismatic personalities of a Catholicism in which, as said above, large numbers of Italians continue to acknowledge a fundamental element of their own identity and their country. Nourished by Catholic imagination, religious television drama in turn gives these people the contemporary televisual version of the sacred ceremonies.

Finally, it should not be forgotten that among the things on our mind, unhappily aggravated by the anxious and turbulent climate of the present, one thing stands out that is harder than any other for the modern individual to bear: the great repression of death, of the finiteness of human existence. Where, then, can one better regain the comforting, authentically heaven-sent fantasy of everlasting life if not in the stories of the immortal figures of religion?

5. The televisual biography

Given Mother Teresa's worldwide fame, the strong appeal of Catholic sentiment and the Italian public's predilection for religious television drama, one would not be mistaken in saying that the success of the miniseries was preordained, or at least amply foreseeable. But we should not for this reason conclude that the role of the text can be overlooked in favour of the overwhelming weight of the extra-textual factors that contributed to the success of television drama. The televisual biography of Mother Teresa was created by a team of very specialized authors and producers; it is in fact a very successful project, which used consolidated Italian expertise to present the miniseries format in two parts, and equally consummate skills to tell stories that could bring together a typically composite and 'cross-sectional' audience. To confine ourselves to the first instalment: the miniseries was watched by viewers of a low educational standard (40%) as well as by graduates (39%); it showed the highest degree of concentration among women viewers (40%), but managed also to attract the male viewing public (30%) and gained a substantial section of young people under 18 (33%), although (as is usual with domestic television drama) it appealed most to viewers over 55 (43%).

The miniseries reconstructs the life of Mother Teresa from 1950 (earlier phases are recalled in flashback): a life that was entirely sustained and guided by her unfailing vocation to caring for outcasts. The narrative draws its inspiration from great simplicity and turns out to be clear and effective, from a didactic point of view, in portraying the missionary ardour of Mother Teresa and her completely trusting surrender to the divine calling. By contrast, certain less well-known traits of the protagonist (played by a well-camouflaged Olivia Hussey), such as the mystic quality of her spiritual experience, the dark and painful zone of her fear, never conquered, of not doing enough to be pleasing to Christ, or on the other hand the grounds for the controversies sparked off by her adversaries, are barely mentioned or merely touched upon.

Respectful and commemorative, the miniseries falls into the genre of religious hagiography. Some television critics have emphasized this with a note of disappointment or of condescension. But however much this view may be shared or regarded as legitimate, we should recall that biographies of saints have based a centuries-old tradition of production and consumption on precisely the old hagiographical models. The televisual biography of Mother Teresa recalls that tradition, still very much alive today, with the additional glamour of an opulent television production.

A gentle breeze, if not one of perfect contentment, redolent of saints' lives recounted in the old-fashioned way, wafts through the miniseries. Together with the luminous photography and the vibrant colours of the indoor and outdoor scenes, against which the white-clad figure of the protagonist stands out in relief, this gentleness helps to make *Mother Teresa* a pleasant and enjoyable production. Accused by some critics of indulging in 'postcard prettiness' or showing India as a tourist destination, the miniseries in fact carefully negotiates the treatment of material that is highly unpleasing to the eyes and the senses – extreme poverty, malnutrition, sickness – softening the impact by means of a decisively soft visual style. Skeletally thin bodies covered in sores, crowds of beggars, the dying bundled in rags, are shown on the scene as an unavoidable yet at the same time slight and discreet presence; similarly the emotional colour of the story is depicted for preference in a light key: it proceeds at a slow and measured pace, even at moments of the greatest dramatic intensity.

Mother Teresa's unshakeable will to follow the divine design of which she felt herself to be the mere instrument – 'a pencil in the hand of God' – comes through clearly. But what emerges more than anything else is her saintliness, showing itself not so much or only in grandiose humanitarian works and religious fervour but also above all in the unequivocal signs of grace that constantly accompany her and succour her, smoothing away any obstacle that might be placed in her path. The way in which, in the televisual biography, all problems are quickly removed and resolved, all opposition overcome, all suspicions dispelled and initially hostile interlocutors won over as allies, is breathtaking and would not be credible were it not for the interpretative criterion of the divine grace hovering over the head of a 'living saint'.

6. A new television event
Co-produced with the United Kingdom and Spain, costing 11 million euros; filmed in Sri Lanka and India with 8,000 extras and an international team of 200 people; followed attentively by the press during the various phases of filming; repeatedly announced and promoted through an intensive publicity drive to whip up expectations – *Mother Teresa* was conceived and realized as a miniseries event. That is how, in the television industry's vocabulary, those productions and more often co-productions are defined which, because of the magnitude of the financial commitment and the wealth of film-making and artistic resources, are head and shoulders above the average production and therefore appeal strongly to audiences by offering outstanding and unmissable rewards. Given its lucrative combination of high productive

values and the guaranteed pulling power of the biography's subject, *Mother Teresa* was bound to be heading for a spectacular success in whichever season it was programmed. Yet it was solely the broadcasting of the beatification ceremony on that exact day that determined the transition of this television drama from the category of miniseries event to the status of a true coronation-style televisual event, of which it became an integral part.

It is clear that a statement of this kind presents problems, in that it does not chime in with the established precepts of media events theory. According to the very rigorous and selective acceptation postulated originally by Dayan and Katz, the definition of a programme as a 'media event' can be applied only if certain essential prerequisites are all met at the same time, namely (the list is not exhaustive) first, the 'live' nature of the event: what is happening must be filmed and broadcast live, in real time; second, extraneousness to the world of broadcasting: we are concerned with 'external' events, independent of the media, where television's part is limited to the transmission; and third, the event must be ceremonial or celebratory, not a routine affair: these events involve planned interruptions, expected and announced, in the flow of everyday life and television programming.

A miniseries event like *Mother Teresa* more than satisfies the last criterion, together with its corollary that the authors call 'norm of viewing' (Dayan and Katz 1992): a sort of sense of duty, if not obligation, a sense of commitment that one cannot or must not shirk (that is what makes a television programme into a 'must-see', which is what *Mother Teresa* presumably was for a fair proportion of its 10 million viewers). Not unlike the genuine ceremonial event, furthermore, the miniseries radiates consensual values that without doubt lie at the centre of society, and not only a Catholic society. And although we should not let our imagination run away with us on this point, the hypothesis of a modality of vision that participates in (even only partially and intermittently) and empathizes with the deferential atmosphere of the performance – the reverential and involved attitude of commentators and participants being, for Dayan and Katz, a pre-requisite of televisual ceremonies – should not be considered implausible.

By contrast, television drama does not satisfy the criterion of extraneousness to the broadcasting world, and still less that of being a live broadcast of an 'external' event. But we would not be doing justice to a theory that welcomes modifications (new forms of ceremony, new ways of filling the public space) if we were to invoke its precepts so as to exclude *a priori* the possibility of reclassifying the televisual events themselves – this would mean, among other things, denying their genre category at a time when even the most rigidly classified genres come up against changes, rewritings and contaminations. Thus one can feel entitled to interpret the precepts more flexibly, to the end of acknowledging and welcoming new variants of celebratory television.

Let us start with the external and independent character of the ceremony. This character is the precondition and necessitates a contractual agreement between the promoters and organizers of the event and the broadcasting institution: an aspect to which Dayan and Katz understandably attach great importance, since the contractual nature of media events and their reliance on a 'pact' between interdependent partners, must depend on the exclusion of unilateral initiatives. But if the substantive key point is the agreement between the parties, all that we know about the ongoing dialogue between Church representatives and Italian broadcasters during the production of religious television drama – LuxVide, producers of the miniseries and specialists in the genre of religion, are among other things very close to the Catholic world – argues convincingly in favour of the thesis that in the case of *Mother Teresa*, even more than in other cases, the pact between religious and televisual institutions must have been clear and strong. As I have noted several times, the decision to programme the miniseries to coincide with the beatification ceremony was taken and announced months in advance, and we can be certain that the Catholic hierarchy were in agreement with the appropriateness of the programming and the script of the miniseries itself. This is testified by the positive opinion of the postulator for the beatification, who previewed the miniseries together with representatives of the missionary order founded by Mother Teresa, and by the presence of high-ranking prelates at the private screening for the civil and religious authorities at the Rome campus of the Catholic University.

If belonging to the broadcasting world can be reconciled with agreement between institutions, the apparently more rigid restriction imposed by the pre-requisite of live transmission lends itself, in turn, to being discussed and reformulated in more inclusive terms. In principle, the media events theory seems to rule out the status of 'event' for any television programme that is not live, which certainly applies to television drama. There has in recent years been an intense critical debate on 'liveness' as a constituent and indeed quintessential property of the televisual medium, the basis of this debate being a pioneering study by Jane Feuer (1983) on the ontology of live transmission as an ideological construct. More recently John Caldwell has defined live television as a 'theoretical obsession' (1995, p. 27), claiming that McLuhan helped to turn it into a legend, while John Ellis, in the context of the discourse on the twentieth century as the 'century of witness', has spoken of a predominant rhetoric of televisual immediacy, aimed at giving viewers an illusion of 'liveness' that is becoming progressively rarer (2000, p. 31). By contrast Jerome Bourdon, while acknowledging that 'the golden age of live broadcasting has long been over' (2000, p. 531), reaffirms the importance of live television: the contact that it gives us with world events, trifling or important, at the precise moment when they happen remains a fundamental part of television's promise and of the public's expectations.

It is essentially to this promise, inherent in the technological potential of the medium – and not to some ontology of televisual 'liveness' – that the theory of media events harks back when it imposes the fetters (or demands the resource) of live transmission of a ceremony, since only live transmission can guarantee the twofold simultaneousness on which the event is structured: being present at the precise moment when the event is taking place and being there when others, unknown to us and far away yet united by the same experience, are present. 'Liveness', wrote Paddy Scannell, 'offers the real sense of access to an event in its moment by moment unfolding. This *presencing*, this re-presenting of a present occasion to an absent audience, can powerfully produce the effect of being-there, of being involved (caught up) by the here-and-now of the occasion' (1996, p. 84).

One can therefore understand and indeed share Dayan and Katz's insistence on 'liveness'. It is not a matter of calling it into question, but rather of exploring the extent of its compatibility with the genre of television drama. To some extent this possibility has also entered the minds of the authors. Dayan (1997b) mentions that he had a long discussion with Katz, at the time when they started to sketch out the theory, on whether they should include television drama programmes of a special nature in the genre of media event – the specific reference was to certain key episodes in *Dallas* – and that they preferred to work on a more circumscribed definition, so as not to dilute the concept. But other scholars have not hesitated subsequently to put forward television drama for inclusion. Elsaesser, for example, has used the phrase 'televisual event' to refer to the German series *Heimat* (1988); Gripsrud reconstructed as an event the broadcasting and reception of *Dynasty* in Norway during the 1980s (1995), and an analogous reconstruction has been made in Italy for *La piovra* (Buonanno 1996). Fiske has convincingly argued that the Murphy Brown-Dan Quayle case has the character of a media event (1994); Morley (1992), more explicitly, has upheld the plausibility of extending the Dayan and Katz model from the rarity of special live events to the more frequent occurrence of those television programmes that are perhaps less exceptional and ceremonial, but in which one can recognize characteristics, potential and functions that are typical of media events in the strict meaning of the term. One can think of the case of *Ramayan*, cited above.

Once again I think that we must look at the substantive meaning of 'liveness' and follow Bourdon's sensible suggestion (2000) that it should be considered not as an intangible absolute, but as a graduated range of variants. The crucial point is the immediate empathy with the event, the privilege of being there – one might say in its presence – when it is happening. In the case of a television drama, being present at the event coincides precisely with the time when it is broadcast. Unlike an external act, which can happen anywhere in the world, there is no way that a television drama can 'happen' except by being broadcast on television screens. This consideration has maximum validity when the broadcast is a premiere. In a programming regime that needs to make intensive use of repeats, the premiere of a television drama – hyped up with ever-increasing frequency through promotional slogans – has the flavour and status of a live programme: for viewers it is a special and unrepeatable opportunity to have access to hitherto unseen pictures and stories when they are revealed on the screen for the first time. '"Liveness" in this capacity thus refers to the simultaneous national experience of a new program, even if it is only the premiere of a new (filmed and edited) episode of *Friends* or *ER*' (Kompare 2005, p. XI). This does not mean that just any programme being broadcast for the first time is suitable for inclusion in the events genre. In the case of *Mother Teresa*, the event-like dimension stems from the ensemble of circumstances that we have already examined, among which can be numbered the specific inflection of 'liveness' that is inherent in a television drama.

'Broadcast in conjunction with the beatification ceremony'. The promotional material circulated from the start of the filming put strong emphasis on the chronological relationship between the religious ceremony, broadcast live during the day, and the drama broadcast in prime time the same evening. In this way it helped to spread the perception and build up the expectation of a twofold aspect, factual and fictional, of one televisual event.

Finally, this new typology of hybrid televisual ceremony does not contradict or oppose the theory of media events – not only because we can accept that some events are not rigidly regulated by the formal precepts of 'liveness' or extraneousness from the broadcasting world, but also for other reasons of compatibility.

Although in principle media events fall into the category and regime of information, as Dayan and Katz observe, they tend to bring about a conversion of news into fiction, or at any rate to blur the lines between the two genres. The narrative course followed by television coverage, the frequent recourse to the repertoire of utopian archetypes and to the key points in fairy stories (one recalls the comparison of Princess Diana's wedding with the fairy-tale wedding of a Cinderella), the appeal to emotions – we find all these in what Dayan and Katz define, not by chance, as the scripts for media events, which together with other similar devices bring about processes of transformation of the events into fiction. The event relates to the ceremony, but the ceremony is likely to be converted into a text of fiction.

We cannot state with certainty that elements of fiction were to be seen at work in the real ceremony of Mother Teresa's beatification. It is, however, certain that the ceremonial moment found its sequel in a text of television drama, and that the drama's imminent programming was incorporated and recalled within the horizon of the religious rite. That is how the television drama became integrated into an atmosphere that was permeated by the vivid memory, or at least the cognition, of the rite celebrated and broadcast only a few hours earlier: in a reciprocal intersection of the ceremonial and the fictional dimensions in a televisual event that was in every sense unique.

4

THE DIGITAL REVOLUTION
OTHER WAYS OF WATCHING TELEVISION

1. A medium in the making

'The key to the future of television is to stop thinking about television as television. TV benefits most from thinking of it in terms of bits' (Negroponte 1995, p. 48). Nicholas Negroponte, a self-declared 'extremist' in predicting technological change, was already in the mid-1990s anticipating a complete reconceptualization of television in terms of 'bits', the unities underlying the universal computer language into which digital technology reconverts information of every type (sound, picture, text, graphics).

I have deliberately quoted an extremist forecaster in order to introduce, by way of a riposte, the appeal to moderation expressed in the phrase 'curb your enthusiasm'. This is an explicit exhortation (which I intend to support in these pages with reasoned arguments) – to moderate the forceful rhetoric that pervades and inspires much of the present-day discourse on the so-called technological 'revolution' in the world of television that is about to come, or is already taking place. Such a revolution is said to have been sparked off in particular by the arrival and relentless spread of digital technology.

Implicit in this exhortation or warning is an invitation to look at the processes of change in the medium and long term, in the empirical manifestations that we can observe in and through social practices within the multi-faceted context of the conditions and forces that cause the changes and orient their evolution. It will be clearly understood that each of the above statements is aimed at a specific critical target and identifies it from among the clamorous and agitated discussions that attend technological innovation. This is how thinking about the duration of the process is set against the presumption of instant rapid change: empirical observation becomes disassociated from abstract and sometimes visionary speculation, and the multi-causal approach distances itself from identifying a single and irresistible technological force of change.

The expression 'curb your enthusiasm' is a quotation, in that it reproduces the title of a contemporary American television series. The series is not so popular nationally and internationally as *Desperate Housewives* or *CSI*, but a fair number of people watch it: it has now reached its fifth season and has acquired a certain following outside the United States. Although *Curb your enthusiasm* (*CYE*) is by no means an isolated phenomenon – I chose it because its title fits my argument, but one could use other analogous examples – a brief reconstruction of its case history will prove instructive for introducing and formulating my discourse on television's new technologies.

CYE is a comedy series of half-hour episodes launched in 2000 on HBO. This premium cable network is one of the leading US pay-TV channels by virtue of the number of its subscribers, now nearly 30 million. HBO has an excellent reputation, both in the States and abroad, for its original television drama, whose high standards of quality and production costs are often accompanied by audacious and original concepts, culturally innovative stories, profound meaning and complexity of form. Series such as *OZ, The Sopranos, Six Feet Under* and *Sex and the City* have received huge critical acclaim, frequent prestigious awards, cult status and at times widespread popularity; they have been exported and have spread beyond the States the unmistakable image of the network, which proudly promotes itself with the slogan 'It isn't TV, it's HBO'. The network is widely acknowledged to have contributed decisively to the advent of a new 'golden age' of American television drama, both directly through its own production as well as indirectly by means of the competition inspired in other networks.

In keeping with the channel's identity *CYE* is a rather unconventional sitcom, though it did not come from nothing. Without being a spin-off or derivative in the true sense, it follows in the train of *Seinfeld*, the terrestrial network NBC's famous comedy that at the height of its popularity in the 1990s attracted an average audience of 30 million viewers; this rose to 76 million for its final episode, transmitted in 1998. Like *Seinfeld* (they share the same author, Larry David), *CYE* can be described as 'a little show about nothing'. In fact it is all about the daily life of Larry David, who plays himself, as do other performers and guest stars of the series, at home, at work and on the streets of Los Angeles. The protagonist is an idiosyncratic and misanthropic character, halfway between self-centred indifference and naïve unawareness of social conventions, laughably inclined to get entangled in the most banal trivialities of everyday life and indulging in behaviour that is as embarrassing and outrageous as it is ill-fated and self-destructive.

Shot on location (not in a theatre or a studio) with a hand-held digital camera, *CYE* dispenses with the soundtrack of applause and laughter that is normally an integral part of the sitcom genre. It restores and exploits a device used by the Italian *Commedia dell'arte*, obtaining unusually realistic performing effects: the scripts of the episodes, although very accurate and analytical in the description of the plots, have no dialogue as such and rely on improvisation by the actors. The result of all these well-conceived deviations from the traditional sitcom is a peculiarly hybrid product, a cross between television drama, fly-on-the-wall documentary and reality show, which gives the refreshing impression of watching live takes of authentic tranches de vie. The fans (the number of viewers of the regular seasonal broadcast has increased to an average of 5 million) and the critics consider it one of the best comedies in American television history, the winner of numerous well-deserved Emmy and Golden Globe awards. Outside the States, *CYE* has attracted a restricted cult following, carved out of the already limited audience of the niche digital channels; in Italy it is broadcast on Canal Jimmy, in the UK on BBC 4.

Like almost all television programmes, *CYE* has numerous websites of its own: the unofficial ones, created and run by fans, and the official one which is part of the HBO site and described as an 'interactive website'. The 'internauts' can find the usual contents on these sites: quizzes to test your knowledge of the series, community forums and on-line shopping, as well as non-interactive sections containing the episodes guide, news about the cast and the programming, interviews with the actors and so on.

If we go through the hundreds of pages that can be downloaded by a research engine by inserting the title, we will find some curious and interesting postings here and there: the complaints from those who feel excluded by not being subscribers from the possibility of enjoying a product whose quality and wit they have heard about. However, the non-subscribers can overcome any such sense of exclusion by purchasing DVDs of the previous season: naturally this act of joining the *CYE* viewers' community must be paid for (the price of the DVD) and requires a digital reader, either free-standing or connected to a television or incorporated in a computer.

The DVD offers unquestionable advantages: complete seasons instead of one episode at a time, contents enhanced by additional information and material (backstage activities, interviews and biographies) that is available in various languages, and above all the freedom to escape the time constraints of the television schedule. The show can be watched at any time and the episodes watched in any order. For those who cannot or do not want to watch the television in the traditional (and in fact still predominant) way, there are other opportunities. Those subscribing to HBO's digital service, for example, are offered what the same channel grandly publicizes as a 'revolutionary new service': HBO on demand. Viewers can bring to their screens and enjoy the best of the network's original series, including the first two seasons of *CYE*, at any time they please.

Lastly, at least for the moment, we have the PVR or Personal Video Recorder. The PVR, first launched in the States under the trade name TiVo, is a digital device. It can be either connected externally or integrated directly inside a decoder, and is capable of exploring a very wide televisual spectrum and of identifying, recording and storing in a capacious hard drive all that is of interest to the user (in the same way as a research engine functions). In Italy the PVR has been incorporated into the latest model of the decoder that is distributed by the Sky satellite operator, who have named it MySky, making the most of the proprietorial status of the user by means of the advertising slogan 'With MySky, TV is truly at your service'.

The official American website proclaims: 'Only TiVo offers you the *freedom* (my italics) to watch your favourite shows anytime.' Among those using TiVo, *CYE* can count on its own viewers and connoisseurs (whose numbers are difficult to calculate) and can help to reinforce the feeling of these connoisseurs that far from being excluded, they belong to an exclusive group of individuals who are capable of organizing 'their own television' by themselves and enjoying it whenever they like. Once again TiVo's advertisement efficiently sums up this prerogative by emphasizing how a PVR widens 'choice and time'.

This quick reconstruction of the case of *CYE* will help us to know where we now stand, and what sort of landscape and horizon we face from an observation perspective in the middle of a technological innovation process that will certainly modify the media environment in which we live. Briefly summarized, the case of the HBO sitcom that I have used as an example leads us to consider a substantial list of recent phenomena and dynamics:

■ The development of the delivery system towards the mixed and branched structure of the multi-channel environment, where the small number of formerly dominant broadcasting networks are joined (in the multiplication of the platforms: terrestrial, cable and satellite) by hundreds of narrowcasting channels, spread by the digital technology of signal compression (*CYE* is produced for a cable network and transmitted in various parts of the world on digital channels);

■ The re-distribution of the former mass television audiences into a range of segments down to the smallest niches, to which viewers assign themselves when presented with the supply of many channels (*CYE*'s audience is one-sixth of that of its progenitor *Seinfeld*, a difference only partially attributable to the intrinsically different characteristics of the two programmes);

■ The use of digital technology during the production and post-production phases, also for ambitious and high-profile programmes (*CYE* is shot with a hand-held digital Betacam, which makes it possible to shoot long external takes at a much lower cost compared to the takes on film, and to obtain all the advantages of this method when it comes to editing, also carried out with a digital system);

■ The diversification of products, in terms of cultural form and content, favoured by the absolute necessity for narrowcasting (which is mainly based on the business subscription model) to capture a public that is willing to pay to have something that they cannot find on the free mainstream networks. Creative talents, attracted by the challenging possibility of conceiving and narrating stories that are more audacious and cutting-edge, have migrated to pay-TV: this is a phenomenon closely linked to the previous one (Larry David went from NBC to HBO and created a sitcom that was probably unsuitable for generalist television and mainstream viewers);

■ The advent of a mode of 'conditional access' to television, where the condition, as previously mentioned, is payment of a subscription or a service (to watch *CYE* you have to subscribe to HBO in the United States or to a digital bouquet in Europe). Pay-TV is not necessarily linked to the digital system, but digitalization makes it possible to extend subscription-based services (consider the case of HBO on demand), and thus the dividing line between the haves and the have-nots;

■ The multiplying of the ways of viewing, either cumulative or alternative depending on the circumstances and the type of viewers. Among the fans of *CYE* there are some who do not miss a single episode on television and some who prefer to watch, or to watch again, several episodes running on DVD. Others who are still more addicted, including those who coined and amuse themselves by repeating the joke 'I can't curb my enthusiasm for *CYE*', may possibly do both. Still others can be tempted by the sporadic or systematic repeats of previous seasons through the services on demand; or some people may decide to confine themselves to selecting on their PVR the episodes that the websites proclaim to be a must-see). It should be emphasized that digitalization supplies the potential for multiplying ways of viewing that are entirely de-synchronized with regard to the temporal organization of the television schedule (a point to which I shall return later);

■ The inter-media cooperation (not to be confused with convergence) that is now established between television and the Internet, with the proliferation of official and non-official websites, chat rooms, newsgroups, forums, games and on-line shopping that are dedicated to a huge number of television programmes. As with *CYE*, the communities of fans can use the Web simultaneously to strengthen the ties to their favourite series and the intra-community ties based on the sharing of such a preference, although the modes and times of watching the programme can only be partially shared, or not shared at all;

■ Lastly, the prevalence, in those promotional discourses that are a remarkable and resonant part of public discourse on technology, of an emancipating vision or ideology that is expressed unmistakably in irrefutable references to the revolutionary conquest of unlimited freedom of choice, apparently in easy reach.

So this is where we stand: faced with a landscape and surrounded by a televisual environment to which we could hardly react, from prejudice or intellectual blindness, by saying that 'there is nothing new under the sun' (Livingstone 1999b, p.60). It is clear from all the evidence that many things have changed substantially over the past twenty years or so and that changes are still taking place. This is disconcerting only for those who, by adhering to an essentialist conception of the television medium, would prefer its assumed 'genetic' and immutable characteristics and ways of functioning and use to be set in stone. But television, as Horace Newcomb opportunely points out, 'has been and is always becoming' (1997, p. XIX). Whether or not this 'becoming' augurs transformations of a revolutionary nature and impact in the near future, to be attributed in particular to the various applications of digital technology, is, however, an entirely different story.

2. Instances of historical amnesia and technological utopia

We must begin by recognizing how easy it is for us to be dominated by 'historical amnesia': we always seem to forget that the advent of new technologies is systematically accompanied by much heralded announcements and predictions that radical change is just around the corner. Emerging technologies have always constituted 'fuel for society's imagination' (Sturken and Thomas 2004, p. 1) – an imagination that is ready to surrender to the spectre of a world turned rapidly and irrevocably upside-down by their impact.

Some twenty years before the present-day enthusiasm for digital technology, which began to manifest itself in the 1990s, American public opinion – as Michael Curtin (1996) reminds us – was gripped by a lengthy and powerful craze for cable television, inspired by the promise of a 'technological utopia of media plenitude' (p. 185). If the promises or indeed the prophesies prompted by technological innovation had truly been destined to become true, then the history not only of technology (peppered with failures) but of the human race itself over the last two centuries would have been – as has been ironically observed (Aarseth 2003) – a 'permanent revolution'.

To emphasize this point certainly does not mean to deny *a priori* and in prejudicial fashion the often substantial and profound impact that new technologies can have in their field and, more importantly, in the field of social behaviour and human experience – even though this can be judged only in retrospect (I shall return to this point). It means rather – and we should be aware of this – that to claim that technology has the capacity to effect immediate, overwhelming, irresistible and dominating change is more than anything an attitude of mind, a point of view or a type of opinion that falls, notoriously, into the category of 'technological determinism'.

'New media technologies emerge, society and human consciousness change in consequence' was Caldwell's succinct and provocative comment (2000, p. 17). Technological determinism is based on a conception of change as a process that is mobilized and guided by a unique or pre-eminent driving force: it assumes and exercises the fascination of explanations that are simple because they are reductionist. The 'fetish' that technology represents in twentieth-century culture and beyond gives it considerable added value and helps to make it into 'an immensely powerful and now largely orthodox view of the nature of social change' (Williams 1992, p. 7).

In reality one should say about technologies what even believers in astrology are willing to acknowledge concerning the stars: that is to say, that they show the way but do not determine it. Or one should say, in terms that are more appropriate in the context of Bourdieusian sociology, that they constitute a 'condition of possibility', necessary but not sufficient, for social change.

Let us consider the case, mentioned above, of American cable television. Its established success, which took at least ten years to materialize, was not simply the result of the introduction of cable as a new technological way of transmitting television signals. In order to account for this achievement, which brought about a reorganization of the American broadcasting industry as well as audiences' viewing patterns, we need to consider other perhaps more potent causes: government policies aimed at impeding the televisual oligarchy of the 'big three' national terrestrial networks (ABC, CBS and NBC); pressure from investors and advertising agencies to break up the television audience mass market into diversified targets according to social-demographic variables and lifestyles, so as to reach them with custom-made and therefore (presumably) more influential advertising (Turow 1997); and the dynamics of differentiating and multiplying individual or group identities, set in motion in an advanced western society like the United States, that revealed needs and requests for cultural products and television entertainment that were similarly differentiated.

Like prejudice, technological determinism tends to stick firmly to denials of empirical evidence (Pickering 2001); and just as prejudice can be positive or negative, so technological determinism tends to demonstrate cultural optimism as much as cultural pessimism. There has probably never been a technological innovation that has not provoked tension between utopia and dystopia, between Panglossian announcements about the coming of the best of all possible worlds and Cassandra-like prophecies of imminent calamity (Bauman 2002. p. 158). But orthodoxy tends to be optimistic in its predictions that a promised land will finally be reached, a Holy Grail finally found. In any case, what has in the past ten years come to be accepted as the 'legitimate discourse' on digital technology is optimistic and full of promises of the freedom to come.

Although the technology-based utopias and dystopias may be diametrically opposed to each other, they and their proponents have in common the same distortion of the time perspective: they look exclusively to the future (it might seem that technological determinism of the dystopic type looks back nostalgically at the past, but it is in fact concerned with technology's malign effects on the future).

There is nothing reprehensible about an attitude that looks to the future, prepares to cope with it and helps to construct it. On the contrary, it shows a commendable, desirable and indeed indispensable far-sightedness on the part of social scientists, media professionals and ordinary people. But the distortion of the time perspective mentioned above needs further consideration: it consists in essence of a perspective of the future that is abstractly *disconnected* from the memory of the past (historical amnesia) and from consideration of the present (that is to say, our present position), as well as being corrupted by the conflation of two categories of time span that in reality are entirely incompatible. These time-span categories are first, technological innovation and its potential and actual applications in tools and services available in the market; and second, cultural and social innovation, correlated with but not automatically dependent on the first category.

Now while technological development tends to proceed quickly and relentlessly, social change – in so far as it concerns the introduction of new technology in the context of everyday lives of ordinary human beings – goes at its own pace, which is normally slower and more prolonged, at any rate on the large scale (Silverstone and Hirsch 1992; Livingstone 1999b). By conflating the two different time spans, the proponents of technological determinism (whether utopic or dystopic; I emphasize again that the former represent the norm in digital matters and it is to them that I wish to refer) not only take it for granted that the future will for good or ill be turned upside down by technology but also, in a fashion that is more myopic than far-sighted, anticipate its coming while assuming that people's lives can change at the same speed as technological development.

Discussions about technology or 'technospeak' (Caldwell 2000), because they do not address the distinction between the potential of technologies and their social consequences, or rather because they postulate a direct and almost simultaneous connection between them, tend to fall into an unavoidable paradox; and most of the current discourse on digital technology is no exception to this. The paradox is the more noticeable in the case of a technology that is assumed to be revolutionary in its nature and impact. It takes the form of anticipating and projecting into a preferably near future something that does not easily lend itself to being anticipated, since it can be observed only with hindsight: indeed it is only with hindsight that it is possible to verify whether and to what extent a new technology or its application has been taken up and incorporated into the usage of members of a population, and has become a feature of their daily lives after having helped to change them. 'We can identify technological revolutions... retrospectively, but it is much more difficult to know when they are in prospect...their consequences have not happened yet!' (Gershuny 1992, p. 228) As Sonia Livingstone also points out (1999b), it is difficult to conduct empirically sound discourses when new technologies are at the starting point; nor is it advisable to make an inference or hazard a forecast based on the pioneering behaviour of the early adopters, who are 'a highly unrepresentative group of the population' (p. 61). A good many predictions on the success of this or that technological application, or on the modalities of use most likely to be adopted, have turned out to be fallacious in recent times: for example, it was thought at first that the VCR would be used mainly as a time shift of television viewing, whereas we know now that it helped to widen the use of home video. WAP (Wired Application Protocol) on mobile phones never caught on, even though great hopes were pinned on this creation that resulted from the much-extolled convergence between telecommunications and the Internet, yet we witnessed the largely unforeseen world-wide success of text messaging. In fact 'the history of technologies is strewn with incorrect forecasts, some of them disturbing, some ironical, many laughable... It is extremely difficult to perceive in advance how important a new technology will prove to be to society' (Sturken and Thomas 2004, pp. 6–7).

Time will tell: this should be our golden motto, to be borne in mind in order to check our tendency to speculate on technologies' potential to transform the future. But this should not justify us in assuming an attitude of inertia or fence-sitting; we should rather consider ourselves under pressure to take up our position knowingly and thoughtfully and to make observations and ask questions from this perspective. This would be a useful and necessary exercise: to recognise the present state of things empirically and cautiously to pick up the signals of possible trends in future evolution, even though they can never be predicted with certainty.

3. A televisual landscape without homogeneity

Let us take another look at the television landscape that emerged from our reconstruction of the case of *CYE* (needless to say, all this refers to the United States and western European countries, without claiming to portray situations in other parts of the world). We must grasp firstly the disparate configuration of a televisual landscape where entities exist that came into being under various technological regimes (analogue, cable, digital), functioning in accordance with various business models (supplied free of charge or on payment); and where even if we limit the field to the digital, we find ourselves confronted by levels of diffusion that vary according to the context and the different applications of the technology.

If by 'digital' we understand, for example, the television channels multiplied by the compression of the signal (DTV), European countries offer a picture of remarkable variety. The rate of penetration of DTV in European households, on average 19 per cent at the end of 2003 (Iosifidis et al. 2005), shows a marked variation between the United Kingdom and Germany: in the UK at least 50 per cent of households have access to DTV (mostly pay-TV), while in Germany the rate is only 5 per cent. Nevertheless in both countries, which like Spain and Greece recently experienced the collapse of a digital platform, the population has access to a multi-channel television environment. There were only five analogue networks in Britain before the introduction of digital, whereas even without the digital, Germany has dozens of analogue channels and still more on cable and satellite. Since one of the much-vaunted advantages of digital technology is its genuine capacity to generate an abundance of channels, the cases of Germany and the United States – the two biggest television markets in the western world – show us clearly that the same objective of a multi-channel environment can be achieved, and has been achieved, by other technologies (even though they are inferior in magnitude and efficiency). From this point of view, the 'revolution' has already been anticipated and digital television – even if we assume a total penetration of the markets – can constitute no more than an extension, an improvement or an overstatement.

As far as the other applications such as DVD, television on demand and PVR are concerned, there seems to be no doubt that DVD – slim, capacious, with enhanced contents – has heeded and responded in a more satisfactory way than VHS to the needs of the fans and collectors of television programmes. Since the widespread diffusion of DVD (just one example: HBO has sold 70 million DVDs of the series *The Sopranos*) is a phenomenon of great importance, we can acknowledge that this specific application of digital technology has had a major impact on the modalities of acquisition and use of televisual content by a significant proportion of the population. But as for on-demand services and the Personal Video Recorder (TiVo or MySky), we must at this stage say 'time will tell'. Both are confined to the circle of the early adopters: the innovators who are curious or who wish to experiment and are highly literate in technological matters. We have already said that it would be imprudent to consider them as being representative of possible mainstream trends.

We should say something about interactivity, another important and much-vaunted promise offered by digitalization. Leaving aside the considerable confusion surrounding the actual concept of interactivity (Van Dijk & De Vos 2001), so-called interactive TV (iTV) is available today in its most elementary forms (electronic programme guide or EPG, choice of camera angle and some other things) but is still in an experimental and tentative phase in the more elaborate versions (opinion polls, voting, games and shopping) which need some sort of return channel, either an external one (telephone, e-mail, text messaging) or, better still, one that is incorporated in the television hardware according to the model of two-way television in its full sense. In both cases, interactivity still has to prove that it is a winner in the field of digital television. In the United Kingdom, the country with the highest rate of DTV penetration in the world, where all Sky Digital subscribers have access to a wide range of interactive services (shopping, banking, e-mailing, betting and other things), only 15 per cent state that they use it at least once a week (Goodwin 2004). Once again, time will tell.

Meanwhile, and to avoid the risk of further historical amnesia, we should bear in mind how cable technology, itself very suitable for two-way television, was obsessed with interactive television well before the advent of digital technology. Without going too far back in time, the last experimental interactive television projects involving cable were carried out in the 1990s: the experiment attempted by Time Warner in Orlando, Florida, where 4,000 families were presented with technological apparatus that could give them access to numerous interactive services, continued until 1997 before being declared a failure, like all previous experiments of this type (Richeri 2004).

One can presume or claim, without any clear empirical evidence, that the television-viewing public look forward to interactive television with a sort of Messianic zeal; or one can conclude, on the other hand, that most people are simply not interested in the idea or the experience of interactive (or more often just reactive or pseudo-interactive) television. There must reasonably be a middle way between these extreme positions. For example, the different versions of interactivity have perhaps not yet managed to conceive and offer propositions that 'satisfy old wants more efficiently or meet newly emerging ones' (Gershuny 1992, p. 232). Perhaps we need to cultivate inventiveness and human creativity more intensely, if we are determined to exploit the interactive potential of digital technology in the televisual environment.

From our present standpoint, therefore, today's televisual landscape appears to be unevenly affected by digitalization and yet undeniably undergoing processes of change. These processes in some instances precede digitalization or are independent of it; in others they represent a well-developed and efficient product; still other processes are at a stage that is too embryonic for their longer-term acceptability to be assessed. The degree of impact that any digital application or other technology may have depends decisively on foreseeing, providing and meeting the expectations and wishes of the public in a user-friendly and attractive fashion. Paradoxically, the enthusiastic supporters of the relentless rise of digital technology seem to be aware of this – but in a distorted manner that conceives technology *a priori* as an efficient response to people's unsatisfied or even unperceived needs, whereas such a response, so far from being accepted as a received truth, should be put to the test every time.

4. From forum to library

A closer look reveals that the changes brought by new technology, clearly seen in the contemporary television landscape, involve two dimensions in particular: the delivery system, fragmented into a plethora of outlets in the multi-channel environment (in parallel with the fragmentation of audiences); and the modalities of television viewing, pluralized in a series of options which all break away from what is commonly called 'the tyranny of the schedule'. Viewers have derived two benefits from this: they have acquired a wider choice of content and more individual control of when and how they watch the programmes.

Having acknowledged the benefits, we must point to some problematical aspects that are connected not so much with costs and requisites for access to the means of choice and control – and, by extension, the so-called 'digital divide' between the haves and the have-nots caused by a number of discriminating factors, not least the level of technological literacy – as to the uncritical adulation that regards both benefits as being liberating, noble and good. As far as choice of content is concerned, we must first clear away the idea that there is a direct correlation between the exponential growth in networks and the expansion and diversification of what is on offer. While the distribution system and consumer behaviour are certainly affected by extensive modifications, this is not (or so far has not been) the case as regards content, or the material on which viewers can exercise their empowered freedom of choice. However much commentators may go on proclaiming that 'content is king', the proliferation of networks and the consequent pressing need to fill them with usable programmes have by no means been paralleled in the production sector. The programming of many minority and niche channels is supplied for the most part by recycled programmes ('more of the same', as people say); and even the premium channels – for which viewers have to make a payment in addition to the standard subscription – are rarely in a position to face the risks and the costs of an original production, once they have added the high cost of cinema and sporting events rights to their budgets.

In this context, HBO and its inventive programming schedule represent a fairly isolated case in the contemporary scene, which is nevertheless worth considering in order to understand what is in store for the television drama industry in the digital television age. Let us go back to where we started, from *CYE*. The series participates in various ways, as we have seen, in the digitalization of televisual products and services, as well as in the now well-known co-operation between television and the Internet; but its most significant relationships with the new technologies are indirect and mediated. These relationships concern the potential of diversifying the cultural forms and content that are being created in the multi-channel television environment. Here we find the enabling conditions (but certainly not any guarantee that it will happen) for the production and circulation of programmes outside the mainstream, made to meet the diverse tastes of the market segments that are targeted by non-generalist channels.

But once the enabling conditions (technological, economic and other) have been fulfilled, the resource that makes *CYE* into a television series that is capable of proceeding to new conceptions of expressive forms is once and for all the human ingenuity and creative talents of the authors and makers. In a digital television world that is crowded with hundreds of channels, such a resource is destined to become more valuable and in demand than ever before, but probably also much rarer, since there are not enough ideas to supply the increasing number of channels with original programmes. Not enough, that is to say, if we wanted seriously to fulfil the much-repeated promise of a cornucopia of programmes, showering forth an abundance and variety of content on which the free or forced choice of viewers could be exercised.

In fact although one tends to take for granted the elective affinity between choice and freedom, removing any possibility of imposed choice, there is only a thin and elusive line between freedom of choice and the compulsion to choose that is generated by a supply-saturated television environment. As pointed out by Ien Ang, the situation of the audience in a multi-channel environment is paradoxically that of being 'condemned to freedom of choice' (1996, p. 13) whether they want it or not.

'Choice fatigue' (Ellis 2000, p. 168–70) does indeed exist; it stems from anxiety and a certain tiredness and impatience, caused by knowing that you have to explore a wide range of options in front of you by looking through specialized magazines or, on screen, the guide to programmes (EPG). These options demand, rather than simply permit, an act of selection (which among other things wastes time), sometimes making the choice 'an imposition rather than freedom' (Ellis, p. 171). Viewers tend to avoid this imposition by deploying their own resources to come to terms with the new environment. In this connection, the systematic reduction of the area of preferences operated in multi-channel homes is well known; in the States, for example, where an average household has access to more than 100 channels, those generally watched number no more than 15 (Webster 2005).

If the conditions of exercising choice are in practice such as to dampen the enthusiasm that greeted the boundless size and the freedom-giving range of available material, we should not allow ourselves to become too entranced by the other aspect of freedom of choice: that which we exercise on time (when we watch) as well as on content (what we watch). For this purpose we have the video on demand, the Personal Video Recorder and the DVD: these are all applications of digital technology, the difference between them being that the technology is incorporated respectively in a service, an implement and a finished product ready for use. They are also appliances that permit the detachment or, to use the word of Giddens (1994), the 'disembedding' of the contents from the time constraints of television programming. You can watch your favourite programme whenever you have the time and inclination: this is the promise that these appliances offer and are able to sustain for viewers whose lifestyles are incompatible with (or who do not care for) the rigid hour-by-hour pattern of television schedules (even though they have been made more flexible by the multi-programming adopted by most of the narrowcasting channels). By making the television usable as an archive or a catalogue, to be accessed according to individual taste and the time available, these devices work as 'disembedding' appliances in two ways: they simultaneously disrupt the embedment of the contents into the context and the logic of the programming, and the collective appointment-like nature of a televisual transmission that is broadcast at a precise and not revocable time slot. In this way the conditions are created of an elective encounter, potentially unique at the moment it happens, between a programme 'taken out' of its proper context and a viewer who is 'isolated' in his or her own viewing.

This may in all probability be the type of free choice that is most likely to appeal to viewers (particularly young people) whose lifestyles are unstructured and do not conform to a regular time pattern. Yet it is true that such a desynchronization of the way in which individuals use television constitutes a break – not wholly benign, perhaps – with the television world that we have known hitherto. That simultaneity of viewing that has made such a significant contribution, throughout the history of the medium, to building up the function of social integration and community maintenance performed by broadcast television, will be considerably diminished by the individualized forms of asynchronous consumption. To 'despatialized simultaneity' we can now add 'despatialized asynchrony', without substituting the one for the other.

But despatialized asynchrony is by no means a new phenomenon: just think of reading a book. Each reader of the same book has read it or re-read it at presumably different times from other readers. In any case the sense of simultaneous sharing of the experience (which I defined as the public character of watching television in chapter I) is not an integral part of reading, nor is it perceived as necessary or valuable. 'Reading is anti-social', said Meyrowitz (1985, p. 124). Nevertheless reading is inseparable from a sense of sharing and connection, even though it is completely detached from simultaneousness. As readers of *War and Peace* or Stephen King's latest best-seller, we know how much we like being part of the community of those who have read or will read the same books: a community that is separated in space and time (more so in the case of a novel that is not contemporary).

The most advanced applications of today's new technologies thus bring us back to earlier modalities of cultural and social experience, and to those that still exist: we shall continue to read books in every television era, just as we continue to experiment with despatialized simultaneity on the wide scale of broadcasting or the narrower dimension of narrowcasting. It may be difficult to pass off transformations of this type as revolutionary; but their role in multiplying the ways in which we enjoy television is not to be underestimated.

Television, as I have emphasized several times, is a flexible medium that can be used in various ways. Digital technology enables us to try out further ways of viewing. Some of these bring us back to the experience of reading and make us think of television not in the abstract and futuristic terms of the digital bit, according to Negroponte's 'extremist' prediction, but in terms of the old and familiar model of a library. This affirmation is never truer than when we refer to DVDs, since they are exactly the same as books, being physical, movable, manageable objects, made to be purchased, used, collected and put in neat rows on bookshelves. They bring into being and preserve the otherwise intangible and fleeting contents of television and introduce a new standard of our relationship with the medium, which is measured in terms no longer of time but of possession of material objects (Kompare 2005) – just as our love of reading is measured by the number of books we own and display on our bookshelves. DVDs are 'television, detached from television and put on a shelf' (Kompare 2005, p.214).

By the end of the 1990s Horace Newcomb had already conceived the hypothesis of a shift in the symbolic meaning and the central function of the television medium: from forum to library. To speak of a shift is perhaps premature; at the same time there seems to be no doubt that the foundations are being laid for 'a vast digital library. The users will enter into these virtual collections just as they go into a library, looking for individual identity and collective affinity' (Newcomb 1999, p. 120).

5

STORYTELLING
THE MULTIPLE REALITIES OF TELEVISION FICTION

1. The television 'super-narrator'

We need to take stories seriously: they are our fairy tales and our myths, our moral tales, the burning fire of imagination whose flame, as Walter Benjamin said, gives warmth to our cold and wretched life. This applies to all the systems and forms of storytelling that have succeeded and joined one another in the history of human society: they have not replaced each other, but from time to time they re-arranged themselves around a central narrative system, which in the second half of the twentieth century undeniably materialized and expressed itself in television.

Every age has invented and narrated its own tales of imagination, in the expressive forms and the media that were available at the time; but storytelling was primarily an oral tradition until the nineteenth century gave life to the novel and saw it flourish to a remarkable degree. This was the century that more than any other craved storytelling, perhaps because it must have given meaning to the experience of incipient modernization (cf chapter VIII). Wherever oral narrations took place, when the stables were closed for the peasants' ball or the squares were opened during the village fairs, they took the form of what we would now call a 'live performance': the narrator or storyteller would tell his stories to the public, who would interrupt and make comments out loud, according to a participatory fashion that has greatly changed, although it has not entirely disappeared nowadays. These storytellers were the successors to the bards and medieval troubadours; they often accompanied their prose or verse stories with music and, like the troubadours, travelled around between fairs and country festivals, if not to courts. This oral narrative tradition has survived up to recent times, although in more and more residual forms; and the novel, despite being periodically dismissed as dead, continues to fill the shelves of bookshops and to produce best-sellers.

But there is no doubt that in the twentieth century it was above all the large-scale forms of media communication, first the cinema and then television, that satisfied the collective need for tales of the imagination. Television met this need, and continues to do so, through a supply of drama that is unprecedented in its continuousness and abundance (it suffices to bear in mind that the national Italian networks, without taking the local and digital ones into account, transmit 10,000 hours of television drama each year, including premieres, repeats and both national and imported productions).

It is not by chance that some commentators have in the past put forward the idea of 'television as our own culture's bard' (Fiske and Hartley 1978, pp. 85 ff), identifying a fair number of resemblances between the traditional functions of the medieval bard and those of our contemporary electronic narrator. Other authors, using less appealing and captivating but more persuasive language, have defined television as the 'central story-telling system' of the present day (Newcomb 1999). Television drama is not the only way in which television fulfils its narrative function – even the news tells a story of sorts – but it is the most relevant and meaningful. We should in fact recognize not simply that television drama is imaginative storytelling but also that it constitutes the most impressive corpus of the stories of today, and perhaps of all time. No other narrative system of the present or the past has ever involved audiences of tens of millions of people, like those who tune in daily to the stories told by the televisual 'super-narrator' (Kozloff 1992).

Nevertheless, perhaps precisely because it is so popular, television drama has been and still is the object of widespread prejudice: many people consider it to be artistically second-rate, intellectually if not morally dangerous and one of the most banal and pointless forms of media production and enjoyment. Even those who watch television drama and derive pleasure from it are reluctant to admit this, for fear of appearing and being 'labelled' as persons of low intellect, limited aesthetic pretensions and easy prey to easily absorbed narrative. This is not a new phenomenon: in the past the novel and literary fiction were regarded as deceitful and mendacious and took a long time to acquire cultural recognition. Furthermore the fact that the cinema now has art form status, and is considered the high-minded 'benchmark' for television, makes us forget that it was the target of intellectual and moral crusades during the early years of the twentieth century.

In truth, stories narrated by television have important cultural significance, however unoriginal, banal and repetitive they may seem (and sometimes indeed are). Television drama offers valuable material for understanding the world we live in. Without faithfully mirroring reality, and without actually distorting it, televisual stories select, refashion, discuss and comment on issues and problems of our personal and social life. Going beyond formulae and genres, language and aesthetics, their fundamental nature is that of 'interpretative practices'. This is how anthropologists define all forms of symbolic and narrative creation, starting with the myths and legends through which human beings in all eras have expressed their own outlook on the world and have given meaning to daily life.

On this last point, the great cognitive psychologist Jerome Bruner – from whom I took the exhortation to take stories seriously, quoted at the beginning of this chapter – affirms in his works the existence of 'a readiness or predisposition to organise experience into a narrative form, into plot structures and the rest' (Bruner 1990, p. 45). Narrative structuring is the indispensable tool for giving order and meaning to the flow of events that would otherwise be chaotic, and cognitively and emotionally out of control. So far from being the prerogative of specialists– storytellers, authors of every sort of fiction, conveyed by every form of media – narrative structuring has constituted and still constitutes a collective resource for mankind. Had storytelling not offered the possibility of reconstructing an intelligible representation of world experience, 'we would be lost in a murk of chaotic experience and probably would not have survived as a species' (Bruner 1990, p. 56). Or, in the words of another writer who takes his inspiration from Hannah Arendt, storytelling is what allows the transition 'from a merely biological life (*zoe*) to a truly human one (*bios*) (Kearney 2002, p. 3).

Order and meaning are created by putting events rescued from the 'murk of chaotic experiences' into sequence and establishing a connection between them (Bruner 1990, p. 56). The capacity of narrative to become an instrument of knowledge and to yield meanings has unquestionably helped to nourish the sort of 'addiction to the story' that seems to have been a universal and ubiquitous constant in human affairs (Kearney 2002). Bruner (2002, p. 27) evokes the eloquent etymology of the word, constructed in turn by Hayden White (White 1987, p. 215): the term 'narrative' originates from an old Sanskrit root – 'gna', meaning 'to know' – which then split in Latin into 'narro' (I tell) and 'gnarus' (knowing). Promoting knowledge, which is understanding worldly things, constructing a comprehensible world and communicating it in the form of a tale: these are the two inextricable values of storytelling.

But narrative covers a vast territory, where one can find everything from everyday conversation (Jedlowski 2000) to journalistic reporting, travelogues, historical reconstructions, novels, pleadings in a court of law, confessions in a reality show and much else besides. The narratives of the world are numberless, as Roland Barthes (1996, p. 46) reminds us.

2. The possible worlds of narrative imagination

For the purposes of the present chapter, which is dedicated to televisual drama, that is to say a corpus of inventive stories for the small screen, it is crucial for us to focus on the distinction – which is to be found in all theorizing about narrativity from Aristotle to Genette to Ricoeur – between fiction and non-fiction, stories that are invented or imagined and stories of things that actually happened. Although such a bipartition may displease not only those who rightly criticize the validity of a polar opposition between fact and fiction, but also the many who more radically claim that one cannot decide between one and the other or that there is now a total post-modern conflation of fact and fiction, nevertheless the bipartition cannot be avoided if one is to recognize the special nature and the unique and precious modus operandi of the narrative imagination.

We can express this dichotomy (which in truth is by no means irreconcilable) in various terms: referential versus non-referential narrative; factual storytelling versus fictional storytelling (Genette); history-telling versus fiction-telling (Kearney); or else by speaking of 'the existence of two large classes of narrative discourse, fictional and historical narrative' (Ricoeur 1984, pp. 81–82). In all these cases we have to make the distinction, already described by Aristotle, between stories that relate events that have happened and stories that relate events *as if* they had happened or might happen. This is the difference between the true and the plausible, the real and the possible. Storytelling of the imagination is the domain of the plausible, the possible, the expression of the 'fundamental human impulse to tell a story *as if* it were happening' (Kearney 2002, p. 9).

There are without doubt crossings, intersections and frequent borrowings in multiple forms between the two categories: historical television drama and dramatized news reporting, fictionalized biography, historical reconstructions resembling great novels, docudrama (Rosenthal 1999), creative non-fiction (Banks 1998) and much else. But however much these combinations may demonstrate that fact and fiction may meet at various degrees of approximation along a continuum, there will always remain a perceptible trace of the original gap between the different 'truth-claims' in the different nature of the proofs that a story requires in support of its veracity. For a factual or historical narrative the 'truth-claim' will inevitably involve the empirical reality: where the events being narrated took place, where the characters depicted actually lived. The veracity or falsity of the story are measured against this external reference point, which is implicitly (or sometimes explicitly) invoked as much by the text as by readers or viewers in those cases where there is an 'interweaving of history and fiction' in the narrative, as Paul Ricoeur says (Ricoeur 1988, p. 180). The narrative may even have recourse, as often happens, to that external reference point, not in order to deviate from the facts but better to carry out its own plan of recounting things that really happened.

This does not apply to fiction, which is free from the shackles of a referential nature, although not from the stringent conditioning of verisimilitude. The credibility of *War and Peace* does not rest on the historical truth of the Napoleonic wars; nor do the book or its readers claim that it did, and nor do we consider that the book is untruthful because it cannot show or refer to any documentary proof of the existence of Natasha Rostova and Pierre Bezuchov. But it is true because it is in the highest degree plausible in accordance with the proper order of symbolic and imagined reality; this somehow incorporates and subjugates the historical-factual element to fictional narrative's primary intention, which without doubt remains the narration of possible reality.

One may protest that the modern tendency to conflate fact and fiction goes well beyond the limits of a nineteenth-century historical novel. But there is no need to accept without question the rhetorical and promotional strategies that seek to portray measured incursions across the frontier, which nevertheless do not change the nature of the 'claim of verification', as major border violations. One can agree that *Big Brother* is fictionalized, but its concept and its success are based on the public display of real people and events which actually happen (or are made to happen). Similarly the simulation of a documentary-style filming of a real event does not take away from *The Blair Witch Project* the freedom of a movie that has no need to prove the existence of a group of boys lost in the witches' wood.

The disruptive force of narrative imagination rests effectively in its freedom to transcend reality. The *as if* is such an essential modality and prerogative of inventive narration because it permits the revelation of possible worlds of life and action where the events being narrated could have taken place and where we could live (and symbolically do live while we are immersed in the story).

Bruner further suggests that stories of the imagination transfigure reality, putting it in a certain sense into the subjunctive (in this connection see chapter III for the theory of media events): that is, the verb mood that expresses a fact or a state as being not real but possible, supposed, desired or feared, as usage and the dictionary confirm. In creating a gap between the world of everyday life – cold and wretched according to Benjamin, impoverished by everyday affairs according to Gadamer – and the world of fiction, stories of the imagination do exactly the opposite of what radical realism (and common sense) reproach them for, that is to say avoiding, or failing to reflect, reality. Television drama is deeply committed to facing reality: it reveals reality's unexplored potential and its perspectives that pass unnoticed, it brings repressed experiences out into the open, sheds light on things we cannot see and anticipates the unexpected that we do not manage to foresee, settled as we are in the repetitiveness of everyday life. Without this gap, this accretion brought to our creative imagination, we would have (and, when the occasion arises, do have) no more than a servile and uninspired reproduction of life as it is lived, according to the most humdrum conception of the mimetic function of storytelling.

The 'subjunctivized' worlds offered to us by narrative invention are not, however, situated at vast distances from the familiar world where we live. Otherwise they would not succeed in seeming true-to-life and plausible to us; we would not manage to see them as possible. Imaginative fiction '[must] alienate us from [real life] sufficiently to tempt us into thinking of alternatives beyond it' (Bruner 2002, p. 94). Sometimes, when the disruptive force of invention seems more real, these imagined alternatives manage to transfigure life as it is lived to a greater or lesser degree, causing the 'seed of subversion' in the narrated life to germinate; and the imagined alternatives work together with cultural and social change in the real world and so contribute to the redefining of shared conceptions of what is normal and what violates the norm.

But even when this does not happen, 'we owe a large part of the enlarging of our horizon of existence to poetic works' (Ricoeur 1984, p. 80), and also the access to a plurality of possible worlds that form an integral part of the multiple realities that inform our life experience.

3. Different life-worlds

'Multiple realities' is a concept coined by the phenomenological sociology of Alfred Schutz, but we need not abandon the world of make-believe to introduce it. On the contrary, we could find nothing better to understand what it is about than a piece of fiction, albeit a very special one: a fragment of Orson Welles's unfinished *Don Quixote*. The fragment is nonetheless fully complete in its meanings, so much so that it has true autonomy as a complete text: it is in fact a perfect epitome of the visionary figure of the knight of La Mancha, in the grip of what Alfred Schutz defines as 'the problem of reality' (Schutz 1964).

The scene is set in semi-darkness in a cinema club; the circle is full of children, while in the stalls, at some distance from the other members of the audience who are wearing modern dress, sits Don Quixote in his knight's armour. Sancho is a few rows away, next to a young girl who gestures to him suggesting the rudiments of 'good audience behaviour' – take off your hat, don't fidget, don't talk – and divides his attention between the screen, where something poignant is going on (Sancho dries his tears with his shirtsleeve), and the distraught face of Don Quixote, who is wincing in such a way as to make his squire worried.

Now the scene on the screen can also be seen: a clash between opposing cavalries of the Roman era, in a place where tall crosses are standing and a young woman is tied to one of them. Don Quixote can no longer restrain himself: he springs to his feet, draws his sword and runs to give the rescuers a helping hand. His slashing blows tear the screen and interrupt the film, while the public in the stalls leave the cinema protesting. But the children in the circle applaud enthusiastically, just as a few moments earlier they applauded the deeds of the heroes on the screen.

This quotation from Welles's filmic fragment here fulfils a function which is particularly illuminating: through the figure of Don Quixote, who in this specific case is revived in a mediatized context, it serves to introduce the central question of the status of the fictional worlds in relation to the world of everyday life, in the context of the theme that we are considering.

But it should first be made clear that we should not take Don Quixote as a paradigm (Montalbetti 2001, p. 125) of the pernicious influence and domination that fiction is presumed to exercise on people's perception of reality (as happens to the character, created by Cervantes and used by Welles, who is deeply immersed in knightly literature or in the vision of it on film and loses all sense of the boundaries between the real and the imaginary). With Don Quixote, we are rather faced with an example of matchless eccentricity, indeed to some extent deviance; this, as we know from Goffman's sociology, would allow greater consciousness of the 'normal' relationships and transitions between fiction and reality.

Alfred Schutz's social phenomenology may prove valuable in this connection. Drawing on William James's observations about the different orders or sub-universes of reality, Schutz (1974) in his essay on the stratification of life-worlds writes of the 'multiple realities' covered by our lived experience: from the world of everyday life, in which – unlike other thinkers, who in turn refer to his model (Berger, Berger, Kellner 1974) – Schutz acknowledges the pre-eminent role of 'paramount reality' , to the worlds of science, art, religion, games, dreams, fantasy or fiction. Each of these worlds, to be understood above all as symbolic worlds, has its own internal coherence and a specific cognitive style that makes it different and contradictory compared to the others. For this reason the transition from one to another of what Schutz prefers to classify as 'finite provinces of meaning', the transition for example from a world of fantasy to a world of everyday life, is never painless; but it is nevertheless a crossing of frontiers that we are normally able to achieve and to recognize. Only an incurable dreamer like Don Quixote – to whom could be applied what Paul Veyne says about cultures: 'There are societies where, once the book is closed, the reader goes on believing, there are others where he does not' (Veyne 1988, p. 22) – is incapable of migrating between the different life-worlds, since his experiences make sense only in the system of meanings that are inherent in the world of imagination.

Let us look again at the Welles fragment; even if it is not directly inspired by it, the scene presents a close analogy with the episode of the marionettes, narrated in what Schutz (1964) considers to be one of the most profound chapters of Cervantes' novel. Don Quixote is watching a marionette show; it portrays the liberation of Melisandra – a Christian lady enslaved by the Moors – by a brave knight. But the two fugitives are followed and when it seems more uncertain what course events will take, Don Quixote decides to intervene: he draws his sword and makes thrusts at the pursuers, destroying the papier-mâché puppets.

The plurality, co-presence and clash between different life-worlds are, according to Schutz, at the heart of this adventure and are treated with depth and intensity. Three regions of reality are simultaneously involved: the knight's fantasy sub-universe, which explains Don Quixote's action (a knight is obliged to come to the defence of a lady in distress); the sub-universe of the theatre, in which the spectator is so deeply immersed in the representation as to believe for a moment that it is real, but where interference with what is happening on the stage is neither permitted nor permissible; and finally the daily life-world, to which the dismembered puppets (or the torn film screen in the Welles version) belong, as well as the request for damage compensation from the unhappy proprietor.

Schutz therefore asserts emphatically that 'it is the meaning of our experiences, and not the ontological structure of the objects, which constitutes reality' (Schutz 1970, p. 252). This is the most interesting point, whether he is referring to the plurality or to the reality status of different life-worlds, including those of fantasy and invention.

I will take up this point, with a slight shift of position. In the Schutz model every world is real so long as we pay attention to it, so long as we are immersed in it (at the theatre, for example, it is Hamlet who is for us the prince of Denmark, not the actor who plays the part), but it vanishes once we move into a different and often incompatible 'province of meanings': the multiple realities are in large measure mutually incomparable and non-communicating. When we shut our book, to quote Paul Veyne once more, we no longer believe. When the theatre curtain falls, we are already elsewhere.

Is it really the case, does it really happen – in particular – that the world of fantasy and invention fades away completely, loses all hint of reality, when faced with the everyday life-world? The question is purely rhetorical. There is no need to adhere to the radical picture of a 'Don Quixote effect' in order to maintain that there are overlapping spaces and yet interaction between the two realities; the imagined is real not only because we let ourselves believe it when we are absorbed, but also because it can intersect with and to some extent modify our everyday life itself, or at any rate the perception we have of some of its dimensions and our way of relating to them.

All this is perhaps more true in the instance of televisual imagination, thanks to the specific modalities of television's presence in our lives. Television is located in our home; and the imaginary worlds that it reveals flow directly and blend with the flow of everyday life, in such a way as to blur the separateness between the two orders of reality. Watching television creates the conditions for more fluid and continuous switching, and for transitions between the real and the imaginary that are less pronounced and upsetting. The accent of reality in television's fantasy sub-universe may be attenuated by transitions that are perhaps never completely removed from the grip of everyday life. Nevertheless it is plausible to believe that this emphasis will retain a more enduring resonance within that reality, since reality and the fantasy sub-universe are constantly intertwined.

4. Widened horizons of mediated experiences

'Narrative...is serious business' (Bruner 2002, p.89). So we need to take stories seriously. One good reason for doing so is that they provide a stage for social reality and organize and display the dramaturgy through which *society represents itself to itself*. Individual stories may have been more or less successful and effective in this respect, just as the modes of representation can be realistic or fantastic, comic or dramatic. But narrating society, representing it to itself, is in each case what narrative systems do.

Storytelling, therefore, is a form of the narrativization of society. We need to look at the quantitative dimension to grasp the importance and the qualitative implications of this statement. Television, in providing material for an enormous volume of production and supply of stories that are directly available at every minute of the day, has done far more than merely appropriate and carry out a function that belonged and still belongs to other narrative systems: it has given rise to a narrativization of society of unprecedented proportions. Raymond Williams had already emphasized this over 30 years ago, in a passage in *Television, Technology and Cultural Form* that is worth quoting almost in its entirety:

> Yet the phenomenon of television drama has also to be looked at in quite another way. In most parts of the world, since the spread of television, there has been a scale and intensity of dramatic performance which is without any precedent in the history of human culture. Many though not all societies have a long history of dramatic performance of some kind; but characteristically, in most societies, it has been occasional or seasonal. In the last few centuries regular performances have been available in large cities and resorts. But there has never been a time, until the last fifty years, when a majority of any population had regular and constant access to drama, and used this access. Even within the last half-century, at the peak of popularity of the cinema, figures for Britain indicate an average of less than one attendance a week per head of the adult population. It is difficult to get any precise comparative figures for television. But it seems probably that in societies like Britain and the United States more drama is watched in a week or weekend, by the majority of viewers, than would have been watched in a year or in some cases a lifetime in any previous historical period... The implications of this have scarcely begun to be considered. It is clearly one of the unique characteristics of advanced industrial societies that drama as an experience is now an intrinsic part of everyday life, at a quantitative level which is so very much greater than any precedent as to seem a fundamental qualitative change. Whatever the social and cultural reasons may finally be, it is clear that watching dramatic simulation of a wide range of experiences in now an essential part of our modern cultural pattern (Williams 1992, p. 53).

It is necessary to dwell on the significance of the availability and accessibility, through television, of a dramatized society. We can see it as a manifestation of a more general and important phenomenon, generated by the constitutive presence of the communications media in the modern world: the profound reconstruction of experience that comes about through 'the tremendous increase', in Giddens' words (1991, p. 24), of mediated experience.

Although it is true on the one hand that forms and ranges of mediated experience have always existed and, on the other hand, that experience lived through in a concrete everyday situation is still of central importance for individuals today, yet there has never been an era that has known a comparable explosion of mediated experiences. A large part of our exploration and knowledge of the world reaches us through the intermediary of major means of communication, primarily television, and unfolds in a very much wider horizon than anything that human beings have experienced in past centuries. There is no need to labour this point, since we are already aware of it, except to state an apparent tautology: in today's world the forms of mediated experience are precisely that, forms of experience in every sense; they are not virtual or escapist pseudo-experiences or simulacra, as some people maintain. We must therefore consider the dramatized and narrativized society portrayed by drama stories on the same basis as an order of reality (symbolically habitable), where it is possible for individuals to have access to new and manifold cultural and social experiences.

In this connection it is worth proceeding more analytically, so as to focus on the specific role of television drama in the processes of mediating experience.

The theoretical reference framework clearly remains what I outlined in chapter I, starting with the discussion of the concept of 'de-localization of social life'. I argued that it would be opportune to reconvert the deprivation of 'no sense of place' (Meyrowitz 1985) into the acquisition of a vast additional resource: the possibility of coming into contact and even becoming familiar with matters, events and places that are spatially far away from the local context where we find ourselves physically, and where our own (always important) direct experiences take place. We no longer need to be 'on the spot' to witness celebrations, historic events (cf chapter III), news stories, natural disasters, moments of public or private life or anything else that may be happening or may have happened outside the localized context of our physical presence. The media, and in particular television thanks to its presence in the home, offers us 'a seat in the front row' (as an effective advertising slogan by RAI used to tell us some years ago) in order for us to be present at and participate in what is happening in places where we are not, where perhaps we shall never go, despite the noticeable mobility of people today.

In this kind of mediated experience there is perhaps a tendency to overvalue the role of information and factual genres and to forget that television drama, with its variety of geographical locations and social environments, human and professional types, intimate and public situations and relationships, opens the door wide to innumerable experiences of dislocation. The Bold and Beautiful acquaints us with the affluent classes living in residential quarters of Los Angeles; we breathe the frenetic nip of the metropolitan air that permeates the detective or hospital dramas set in New York, Las Vegas and Chicago; and, without travelling too far, Italian viewers experience provincial Italy through stories such as Marshal Rocca or Inspector Montalbano, and are transported to Naples when they watch the soap A place in the sun or the detective series The crew.

Being able to benefit from such mediated dislocation entails much more than wandering between various more or less remote places without moving from one's own home or armchair, although this experience of 'imaginary tourism' or travel without a departure is not to be undervalued: it makes the most sedentary individuals or viewers mobile in the virtual sense. It can also be the origin of real journeys and material displacements, as happens when a place is made famous by a television drama and attracts hordes of visitors. Nick Couldry (2002) speaks in this connection of true 'pilgrimages' being undertaken by 'media pilgrims' who are fired by the wish to pay a visit in person, going to the actual spot, to the setting of a drama that they know well – in a case studied by the author, the setting in Manchester for the very popular soap opera Coronation Street. For the viewers who are most absorbed and involved, the visit can take on the character of a ritual occasion, the background to a memorable and perhaps unrepeatable connection between two life-worlds: the ordinary world of everyday life, where Coronation Street is a televisual commitment inscribed in the domestic routine, and the out-of-the-ordinary world of the televisual story factory, experienced by means of the unique or rare opportunity to be physically present in the actual place where the soap was filmed and brought into existence (not by chance, all those interviewed waxed lyrical about the exciting sensation and indeed the privilege of *being there*).

But beyond the spaces of physical geography it is situational geography, to go back again to Meyrowitz, that is greatly enlarged by the possibility of undergoing dislocated experiences; as we sit in front of the television screen we are witnesses and participants of the widest range of social situations that unfold in a multiplicity of environments and present a plurality of topics and behaviour, both personal and professional, of a type and quantity that it would be difficult if not impossible to encounter and observe in the normal run of everyday life. Precisely because television drama is a narration of society and portrays many more aspects of it than other televisual genres, it acts as a powerful 'widener' of the range of social situations to which we have access without being physically present at them. We can observe a trial in a courtroom drama, follow the process of the investigations in a detective series, be admitted behind the scenes of the medical profession in a hospital drama, and enter into the intimacy of the home and personal relationships in a soap.

In turn we establish personal relationships; these are based on a sort of one-sided and non-dialogue-based rapport that Horton and Wohl (1956), later taken up by Meyrowitz (1985) and Thompson (1995), had already identified in the 1950s as a distinctive characteristic of mediatized society and defined as 'para-social interactions'. They are the interactions that members of an audience develop (from a distance, and unreciprocated) with media personalities, television show hosts, actors and artists. These are secularized bearers of the gift of ubiquity, obtained thanks to the presence of the television set in millions of homes, and convey the illusion that each individual viewer can meet them at close range, almost face to face. These constant, sometimes daily, meetings within a symbolically shared space can cause viewers to feel a familiarity and even an affectionate attachment towards the television personalities; they feel that they know them intimately, they have imaginary conversations with them and address them out loud. Some of the personalities end up by being perceived as true friends, 'media friends' in fact (we have already come across this concept in chapter III: Meyrowitz 1985).

It is symptomatic of the sneering attitudes towards the impact of television on the experience of everyday life that have prevailed from the beginning that the unquestionably sharp intuition of Horton and Wohl (1956) should have cropped up in a pathologizing discursive context. The authors perceive in para-social interaction the 'simulacrum' of an authentic conversation, of a true relationship which could be developed, and assign to this interaction a 'compensatory' value for the type of viewers who are socially deprived: people who are lonely, elderly, ill, marginalized or disturbed (it was perhaps not by chance that Horton and Wohl's essay was published in a psychiatry periodical). Meyrowitz in truth emphasizes how this new form of interaction is also to be found 'among average people' (1985, p. 120). But para-social interaction remains branded by the stigma of 'mild psychic disturbance', a stigma that John Durham Peters quite recently urged should be removed (2006, p. 120), recalling that non-dialogue forms of communication are not necessarily abnormal or imaginary. For Peters, who (as we have seen in chapter I) does not hesitate to spin out a convinced and convincing encomium of the communicative model of 'dissemination' that is typical of broadcasting (Peters 1999), the imagined relationships that many viewers establish with television personalities seek above all to give the lie to the supposedly impersonal character of so-called mass communication; and although the relationships constitute a new type of affectionate and intimate link, cultivated far away from and even unknown to its object, they are not in essence entirely different from many equally non-dialogue and non-reciprocal relationships that one happens to entertain during one's life, even in relationships involving proximity and face-to-face contact. 'Para-social interaction is only the tip of the iceberg' (Peters 2006, p. 120) of the absence of reciprocity, embedded in numerous aspects of our culture and not lacking in a certain necessity and sometimes 'nobility', to quote Peters.

Concerning more specifically the theme dealt with in these pages, I want to introduce a consideration – generally glossed over or neglected – on the symbolic device that arouses and supports the phenomenon of 'media friends': it is, looked at carefully, the 'as if', that perceptible and precious gap between what is true and what is plausible, the real and the possible, that confers on imaginative narrative all its power to transfigure the world. Such members of the public as maintain a para-social rapport with televisual personalities and characters, no matter whether to fill up affective and relational vacuums in their lives or to forge a sense of belonging and communication (think of the conversations between the regular viewers of a serial or a reality show), behave 'as if' the objects of their interest and involvement were near by, known and available, whereas they are in fact far away, unknown and unreachable. Seen in this light, establishing a personal connection with entertainers, characters, television artists and media celebrities – even when they are, so to speak, encountered and 'met' in the framework of factual or entertainment programmes – always entails sticking to a make-believe regime of 'suspension of disbelief', which makes the friendship with perfect strangers credible, practicable and not infrequently engaging and gratifying.

But however engaging it may be, the para-social relationship – precisely because of the absence of reciprocity and dialogue – is not binding, as is a relationship of any sort with other people to a varying degree. Media friends do not demand the commitment, not always given willingly or gladly, that is a feature of a real-life friendship; nor do they complicate our lives with the problems that are inherent in keeping a relationship in existence. 'TV not only provides me with "company", but it also causes me to react mentally, and, therefore keep emotionally active, *without having to face any consequences*' (my italics: the statement is recorded in Gauntlett and Hill 1999, p. 115). Just as the specificity of the domestic environment where television is normally watched loosens or indeed breaks the prescriptive and proscriptive norms of behaviour that 'befits' a particular occasion (cf chapters II and III), the specificity of para-social interaction frees those who engage in it unilaterally from obligations and prohibitions; in short, from the set of rules to which a purely elective human relationship is always subjugated.

What happens, thanks to para-social interactions, is an extension and an enrichment of the personal capital of social relationships, and an intensification of the experiences of relationship: a process in which television drama plays a primary role, in no case inferior to that played by the entertainment genres or to the talk shows, since the storylines of television drama put viewers in contact – frequent and prolonged, thanks to the serial formulae – and favour interaction between the largest possible repertoire of human figures. The community of soap opera characters, whom viewers 'meet' every day, or the recurring heroes of the weekly series are liable to become companions and friends, closer than our neighbours, and to constitute reference points and terms of comparison for formulating our life choices, and to produce instances of impassioned loyalty and individual and collective devotion to the 'cult'. Let us note, for example, in the research carried out by Dominique Pasquier (1999), how adolescent fans of the French series *Hélène et les garçons* find in the television drama and its protagonist a guide on finding one's way through the still unexplored territory of romantic love, relations between couples and feminine identity; and what a massive volume of intimate correspondence they address to their favourite heroine through the television network, without falling into the trap of naively identifying the fictitious character with her real-life portrayer. 'Why should anyone think they are suffering from a dangerous delusion?' the author comments. 'After all, isn't it precisely the proof of television's capacity to carry people, emotions and affections over long distances?' (p. 92)

Just as media friends are often chosen from among the characters and actors in television drama, either domestic or foreign, it is equally through television drama that in large measure we find those contacts mediated with the rare experiences spoken of by Giddens (1991, p. 27 and 168). So as to introduce and sustain a widespread sense of 'ontological security', which is vitally important in preventing modern society from being overwhelmed by existential problems and moral dilemmas, an entire ensemble of fundamental components of human life – Giddens maintains – must be set aside, in a sense 'sequestrated' from the routine of everyday life. Folly, criminality, illness, death, sexuality and nature, to the extent that they constitute the main areas to be thus sequestrated, thus become – unlike in pre-modern societies – 'rare experiences', removed from our sight, often hidden away in custodial institutions (asylums, prisons, hospitals).

However, the rarity of direct experiences becomes markedly weakened by their frequency in mediated experiences: information, the cinema, television and every form of narrative genre abound as never before in stories and pictures of sex, violence and death. These media items, which are often the object of hand-wringing and moral crusades, keep us in constant contact with uncommon experiences. They also help to keep awake, maybe even to enrich, our existential sensibility when faced with the most problematic areas of human life – this in a fashion that by availing itself of the immunity of mediated experiences (immunity from the risk of direct involvement) does not encroach substantively on our sense of ontological security. One could say, without attaching any generalizing importance to such an affirmation, that mediated contact with sequestrated experiences subsumes the conditions for neutralizing insecurity: still more so, probably, when this happens in the context of the regulative and productive structures of the meanings of television drama stories.

The mediating function of television drama certainly seems particularly relevant in relation to illness, crime and death. It is on these areas of experience that some of the main genres and the most popular ones are based: detective dramas, hospital romances, action dramas. The painstaking counting of the crimes or violent deaths that recur, for example, in the daily or weekly programming of series or serials does not perhaps meet its declared purpose – measuring the amount of violence shown in order to infer its effects on behaviour – but proves how the worlds of television drama are widely permeated with experiences that are sequestrated from the reality of everyday life.

Access to social settings that are far removed in space and time; interaction with personalities one has never met in person; contacts with fundamental areas that are concealed from human life; we come back, in conclusion, to the 'vast range of experience' made possible for today's public by the televisual practice of narrating society, spoken about by Williams, and to the multiple realities that were revealed by the social phenomenology of Alfred Schutz.

By the same route, thanks to the expansion of the horizons of mediated experience that are disclosed by the largest narrative corpus in historic memory, television brings 'an increase in being in our vision of the world which is impoverished by everyday affairs' (Gadamer, quoted in Ricoeur, 1984, p. 81) and contributes significantly to the pluralization of the possible worlds created by narrative imagination.

6

The Paradigm of Indigenization
Beyond media imperialism

1. Paradigms revealed

The purpose of this chapter is to consider and re-examine an issue that has been a 'classic' topic since the 1960s for debate in the field of media studies: international television flows, with particular reference to the import and export of fiction programmes.

I must first note that this issue is a key component of the system of relations between 'us' and 'the other,' regardless of the terminology adopted to express this basic dichotomy: 'domestic' versus 'foreign,' 'national' versus 'international,' 'local' versus global.' In particular it hinges on and is caught up in the same perceptive and discursive patterns that shape the discussion on the nature, dynamics and outcomes of encounters between different cultures (or aspects of different cultures), in this case those relating to media and television. We thus see how the issue pertains to the area and problems of inter-cultural relations.

I shall turn in the next chapter to the theme of international televisual flows in the context of inter-cultural encounters, seen from the perspective of travel theories. This chapter will be dedicated to a critical examination of the main interpretative model offered by scholarly literature regarding the international circulation of television programmes: the paradigm of media imperialism. For this purpose I shall adopt an alternative theoretical model, which I shall define 'the paradigm of indigenization'. (It should be understood that in both cases we have a contractual definition, a sort of convention that is internal to the present discursive context, rather than a strict and legitimate application of the concept of the paradigm.)

John Tomlinson, author of a study on cultural and media imperialism that shows admirable acuteness and analytical depth, considers that the huge corpus of texts that deal with the issue do not contain a coherent ensemble of ideas to a sufficient extent for them to be regarded as an 'approach' or a 'thesis' in the proper sense – although these formulae are commonly used, the same as 'model' or 'paradigm', to refer to them.

The discourse on media imperialism has given rise to an abundant and influential theoretical and empirical corpus of writings (Schiller 1969, 1976 and 1991; Tunstall 1977; Boyd-Barrett 1977; Mattelard 1979; Varis 1986; Septstrup 1990; and for a meticulous critical introduction Tomlinson (1991), whom I have already cited). This contrasts with what is sometimes known as the 'hypodermic' or 'magic-bullet' theory, which never actually existed (Wolf 1992) as a scientific construct that was consciously elaborated or accredited in academic literature. The reference is pertinent, since the whole 'hypodermic' conception of media power is an organic part of and falls under the discourse of media imperialism.

Media imperialism originally emerged as an articulation of cultural imperialism; but the fact that it attracted all the attention and ended up substantially by marginalizing the most comprehensive concept of cultural imperialism, constitutes firm evidence of the media-centric slant of the discourse – a slant that has been strongly emphasized by Tomlinson. Like the word 'imperialism', it instantly makes explicit the 'thesis' of an influence, an instance of cultural domination, exercised by nations or hegemonic systems on the world stage of politics and economics: the United States, capitalism, the West.

The theory of cultural domination was originally formulated in the second half of the 1960s. Reconstructing its genesis twenty years after the event, its first and most authoritative proponent, Herbert Schiller (1991), traced the theory back to two pre-eminent characteristics of that historical period. One of these was the imbalance of force and power between the largest geopolitical areas of the world, separated as they were by a deep divide (especially between the West and the Third World) in terms of economic and industrial development, technological systems and living conditions. In this scenario the United States stood out as the most powerful state of the first, and therefore of the whole, world. The other striking characteristic was the 'rapid development of television and its capability for transmitting compelling imagery and messages to vast audiences' (1991, p. 14). The close convergence of interests between the economic and the cultural sphere caused American cultural products, especially television, to spread to the greater part of the planet and to follow in one direction: from the centre to the periphery of the empire, described as the 'one-way flow of television' (Nordenstreng and Varis 1974).

We can turn to John Thompson (1995) for a brief exposition of media imperialism. I reproduce here the passage, almost complete, concerning the American 'electronic invasion'

> The dependence on American communications technology and investments, coupled with the new demand for TV programmes and the sheer costs of domestic production, have created enormous pressures for the development of commercial broadcasting system in many Third World countries and for the large-scale importation of foreign mainly American programmes. The result is an "electronic invasion" which threatens to destroy local traditions and to submerge the cultural heritage of less developed countries beneath a flood of TV programmes and other media products emanating from a few power centres in the West. These programmes are infused with the values of consumerism,...through which individuals are harnessed increasingly to a global system of communication and commodity production based largely in the US (1995, p. 166).

Americanization, consumerism, destruction of local culture: the most remarkable aspect of media imperialism is that its cornerstones are in equal measure the pillars of contemporary common sense. Even without ever having heard of media imperialism, many people would subscribe to the opinion that there has been an advancing homogenization of cultural values on the planet, under the invasive impact of the consumerist values disseminated by American cinema and television.

Without presuming any direct familiarity with the specific formulae and texts concerning media imperialism on the part of many people outside academic circles who adhere to and (even unconsciously) share this theory, we obviously face the somewhat uncommon instance of the coincidence between two different types of discourse: on the one hand, the academic and specialist, and on the other, the inexpert and common: broadly speaking, from political or journalistic discourse to everyday conversation. These two levels of discourse bring into play (albeit at different levels of intellectual elaboration and the sophistication of the argument treated) the same set of ideas and prejudice, in claiming that the Americanization of cultures (not only televisual one) is an incontestable reality.

Yet things change, whether in the mutation of the phenomena under observation – due to the variability and evolution of factors and circumstances that produce and shape them – or in the shift of perspective from which these same phenomena are observed. The geopolitical scenarios, the landscapes and the televisual systems are in many parts of the world no longer those on which the theory of media imperialism was based in its day. The theory has been called into question in the light of different theoretical approaches, and by a considerable corpus of empirical research on television reception. The theory's sympathizers have yielded to 'legions' of critics, as Marwan Kraidy has provocatively remarked (2005).

On the other hand the changes, in whatever field they occur and therefore also in both media and media studies, rarely give rise to wholesale substitutions, at least in the short and medium term. Substitution is rather an interpretative category which we tend to apply willingly because it simplifies things. The paradigm of media imperialism, challenged and tested by the new state of things and new approaches, has lost its central position in the field of explicit theories, but still maintains its hold at the level of the implicit theories that underlie public discourse and ordinary conversation.

At the same time, the paradigm itself has been revived by, and seems imperceptibly to pervade, the alarming predictions about a homogenized transnational metaculture, which a widespread myth-making tendency (Ferguson 1992) now attributes to globalization. 'What replaces imperialism is globalisation', Tomlinson warns us (1991, p. 175). For his part, Herbert Schiller acknowledges in the work already referred to (1991) that there have been numerous changes in the geopolitical map of the planet since the theory was first formulated – in particular the considerable reduction of United States power in the face of growing cultural domination by the big multinationals. However, he has repeatedly pointed out the lasting and indeed reinforced role ('heavier than ever', p. 15) played by television in the field of culture and has concluded that we are 'not yet in the post-imperialist era'.

The situation may seem very confused and is indeed more complex than schematic visions and dogmatic paradigms would have us believe. I therefore have no intention in the rest of this chapter of simplifying phenomena which are by no means simple. I will try rather to shed light on the more complicated and less predictable developments and processes that have been brought about by international television flows.

I maintain in particular that Americanization is neither inevitable nor permanent, and that in any case the question has been exaggerated, especially as regards its 'effects.' I also maintain that local cultures retain a strong influence on television consumption and production, within the globalization phenomena. Finally, I suggest that in television, as in any other cultural field, contacts and relationships with foreign forms and products give rise in most cases to new forms and products that are at the same time hybrid (Garcia Canclini 1989; Pieterse 1995 and 2004; Kraidy 2002 and 2005), original, and sometimes unmistakably home-grown.

2. Going native

'At least as rapidly as forces from various metropolises are brought into new societies, they tend to become *indigenised* (my italics) in one or other way', states Arjun Appadurai (1990, p. 295) at the beginning of an essay that has become an authoritative and almost indispensable reference point for anyone who is working with and thinking about globalization, inside or outside the field of media studies, from perspectives that do not take increasing homogenization for granted but are at pains to acknowledge the unceasing processes of cultural heterogeneization (Hannerz 1990; Thompson 1995; Lull 1995; Sinclair, Jacka, Cunningham 1996; Tomlinson 1999; Berger and Huntington 2002; Pieterse 2004).

By the concept of 'indigenization' I mean the process through which forms and expressions of external cultures, elaborated by other societies, are appropriated, re-elaborated, and restored by diverse local societies in configurations that are consistent with their own home-grown systems of meaning. This process gives rise to forms and expressions which in their hybrid and syncretic nature are the result of a mixture of native and non-native elements. They are visibly marked by domestic specificity and represent original and authentic creations of local culture.

A concrete case might be clearer and more convincing than an abstract definition. Take, for example, the 'spaghetti western', whose hybrid nature appears in the very name. It is the Italian rewriting of the most American of all cinema genres and a vivid and eloquent example of how intense contact with elements from a different culture offers resources to, and creates the conditions for, the production of new formulae and genres. The 'spaghetti western' is not the mere repetition or imitation of an imported model, but transforms the non-local material, providing new configurations of an unmistakably local taste. It is the result and can serve as a paradigmatic example of indigenization, and of the multiple cultural differences which this process is likely to produce. However, it is in no way exceptional. For instance, the process of indigenization is at work in Neapolitan 'posse', played to a rap beat; in pizzas and hamburgers served up all over the world but garnished with local ingredients; and in the international circulation of television formats adapted to different national peculiarities. Numerous other cases could be mentioned.

To sum up then, the fundamental difference between the paradigm of media imperialism and that of indigenization is this. The former postulates that national and local cultures exposed to foreign media products risk being suffocated in a deadly stranglehold. Their specificity is diluted as part of a process of homogenization, which flattens them out according to the (American) cultural models that dominate the world. The paradigm of indigenization is different: the unbalanced and asymmetrical positions that are nearly always a feature of inter-cultural relations and an undeniable given of the global expansion of the American product do not detract from the fact that locally situated cultures are able to appropriate and transform models and meanings of foreign origin and reconstruct 'localized' and heterogeneous versions or variants.

It is worth spending a little more time on the premises, presuppositions, different assumptions and ideas that inform these two different paradigms and are reflected in their respective terminologies. The vocabulary of imperialism speaks of cultural domination and dependence, ideological control, colonization, imitation and homogenization, whereas the vocabulary of indigenization includes asymmetry, interdependence, appropriation, hybridization and heterogeneity.

Three major inter-related levels of discrepancy must be considered. They concern theories of communication, the definition of what is local and what is global, and the understanding of their mutual relationship.

One of the reasons why the paradigm of media imperialism, or a not too dissimilar theory of globalization, has been so widely accepted, even by the public at large, is probably that it is based on a communication model that is in its turn widely accepted, and indeed taken for granted: the transmission model. According to the transmission model, communication consists of messages sent – by means of a given medium or channel – to a recipient. As the name itself indicates, the subjects in this process hold very unequal positions: the one who sends is active, the other is passive. Inherent in the model is the idea that the message incorporates the meaning intended by the sender, and that the recipient (the public, the audience) automatically accepts it and is influenced by it, although resistance or refusal by the audience is not excluded as a residual possibility. In this simple, linear way, communication achieves its ends and exercises persuasion and control, as well as imposing ideology and culture.

For a long time, theories about the influence of the media were based on this transmission model of communication. Indeed, public discussion continues to refer to it. Take, for instance, the controversy over violence in the media, or television and children. This model gains credence because the relationship between media and audience that it proposes is transparent and makes things simple. The paradigm of media imperialism and current discourses about globalization share the same perspective in stating that exposure to American products inevitably leads to the Americanization of local cultures, and claiming that a large-scale process of cultural homogenization is under way worldwide, caused by the planetary expansion of American culture – in terms of not only the media but also eating habits, consumption in general and leisure activities.

The dominance of the transmission paradigm has in relatively recent times been undermined by the 'ritual model' of communication (Carey 1989). According to this model, the communication process – far from coinciding with a mere transfer of preconceived meanings – is rather to be seen as an interactive and dialogic practice by which and through which meanings circulate, are exchanged, interpreted, negotiated, transformed and possibly shared.

The notion of sharing, which is in fact inherent in the very etymology of the word 'communication', as something which is experienced in common or in communion (the archetypal example is the religious ceremony), is central to this model. It is also central to this discussion, in that it radically redefines the conditions and calls into question the possibility of a common or even global culture. A culture of this type does not lend itself to being conceived as the result of a mere transmission or imposition of meanings. The meanings themselves have to be shared by the social parties, whether individual or collective, who are involved in the communication. This cannot be taken for granted or asserted *a priori*. (It is difficult, indeed no more than conjecture, to affirm that the audiences in dozens of countries share the same culture simply because they watch the same programmes, such as *Emergency Room* or *Desperate Housewives*.)

What is equally central is the identification of the communicative process with a process of symbolic production. The ritual model agrees with the approach of 'the social construction of reality' (Berger and Luckmann 1966) and stresses the active and interpretative nature of communication, making it the 'site' where culture and reality itself are preserved, regenerated and transformed. The paradigm of indigenization has obvious similarities with the basic suppositions of this theory, in the emphasis placed by the model on the inexhaustible cultural productivity of communication.

As regards other divergences, part of the paradigm of imperialism, and, once more, of current opinions about globalization, is the dichotomy between what is local and global, and between the values associated with these respective concepts. Being conceived as two static and opposite poles, the local and the global they take on essentialistic and irreducible qualities. The former corresponds with originality, purity and the expression of true identity and represents the positive but also weak and vulnerable pole. The latter represents the non-authentic, the fake, the false identity, epitomizing the strong, aggressive and confusingly intrusive pole. This definition of the two terms leads to a conception of their relationship that emphasizes the invasive power of the global, and considers resistance and protectionism as the only practical way of safeguarding the cultural roots of the local.

Seen from the perspective of the indigenization paradigm and its assumptions, the same elements take on, in their respective contours and reciprocal positions, a different, more mobile 're-combining' configuration, in which the trajectories leading to and departing from temporary destinations are visible. That which at a given moment may seem to be the uncontaminated expression of local culture, may in the end turn out to be the result of an earlier contamination with external cultural elements, which could prove to have been invasive. For example, how many genuinely local elements of Sicilian cuisine or dialect are Arab in origin? Or again, how much of American culture comes from Europe? The local and the global are by no means pitted against each other as opposite poles in a bi-polar cultural universe: they intersect and interpenetrate, the one expressed in the other. There is no culture, except a totally isolated one, that does not incorporate 'a different mixture of "alien" ideas' (Robertson 1995, p.41). And today (without wishing to deny or exaggerate conditions of inequality in power relationships) this applies no less to so-called global culture than to local cultures.

On the subject of aliens, we find in the final work in the film quadrilogy *Alien* (*Resurrection, 1997*) an eloquent metaphor for this idea. Lieutenant Ripley has been impregnated by a monster and becomes mother to a monster, as she herself says. She is a clone and so a hybrid creature, part superhuman force and cleverness, and part human compassion and maternal tenderness. These elements of identity mix and recombine in her to create a new and different incarnation of 'our' galactic heroine. At the same time, the film expresses all our phobias regarding hybridization, and shows us the horrible forms of nightmarish beings created by experiments of genetic contamination between humans and aliens.

Psychologically and culturally, it is extremely difficult for us to recognize, let alone accept, that 'the other' can take root in us and become part of our own identity. If the paradigm of indigenization goes largely unacknowledged in wider circles of public opinion and the implicit theories which inform public discourse, that is not only because it is a complex and thorny question, but also because it encounters these difficulties and this resistance.

Many of us have no doubt experienced discomfort on making the unexpected discovery that we too are 'native.' Adolescents tend to read lots of books with the common feature of exotic settings. These include stories of adventure, travel and geographical discoveries. Such tales of far-away lands afford 'escape without departure' and generally include 'natives,' that is the indigenous local population. One often encounters the intractable misunderstanding that 'native' denotes members of races and cultures unlike our own, generally more primitive and less civilized than we are. The 'native' becomes synonymous with the 'other'. Sooner or later the ambiguity is cleared up by our teacher or the dictionary. We discover that we too are 'natives', and the discovery leaves us perplexed. With good reason: we have not only discovered the correct meaning of the word, we have also discovered that it applies to and defines us, while we had believed that it was our definition for others. Thus in a small way and with some disbelief we find ourselves different, *changed*, because we can call ourselves by the same name that we use for others.

In terms of individual self-perception, this very common experience is equivalent to a process of indigenization and it summarizes the meaning of the process: we become native, and we do so through some form of contamination by the other.

3. Supply: the media are American
I now intend to take an analytical approach to certain questions that have given rise to opinions which are actually very confused, in spite of their apparent crystalline certainty. This confusion derives largely from its near-synonym 'conflation': literally, mixing together different materials and elements. In other words, conflation is the opposite of keeping things distinct and separate.

As regards globalization and our particular focus on the Americanization of televisual preferences and cultures, the conflation and confusion are at three different levels, which are analytically and empirically separate: the respective levels of distribution and supply, consumption and success, and influence and effect. Each of these incorporates different phenomenologies and different forms, measures and meanings of Americanization; none of them corresponds precisely with what popular, alarmist and reproachful usage intends by the term.

The supply level refers to the presence of American programmes on television channels almost throughout the world. The extent of this presence varies, according to the examples, but is considerable. An average of 50 per cent of films and television drama on terrestrial networks in European countries is of US origin (Buonanno 1997–2006).

Traditionally, and in large part still today, the international circulation of American products takes place by means of importation, or rather the broadcasting rights are acquired by national television stations and networks. More recently, extended circulation and new flow channels have been opened up by satellite technology, allowing big American and (and other) providers to distribute their products directly.

In general, the multiplication of television channels – limited, as has been seen with the advent of commercial television, or exponential, as has been made possible by digital technology – brings with it an increased reliance on American products in programme scheduling. The reasons are essentially the same for broadcasting and narrowcasting (which we will examine later). These include wide availability, relatively low costs – although costs tend to rise in a scene of ever-increasing competition – and a guarantee that they will be well received by viewers, even if they are not a success.

To ascribe the widespread, even definitive Americanization of television programmes worldwide to the advent of multi-channel television would be an over-hasty conclusion. The picture is actually much more volatile and complicated. The proliferation of television channels takes place within television systems that, like any other complex environment, are characterized by asynchronies and by the simultaneous presence of formations at different stages of development, which require different strategies and resources. Newly arrived niche channels co-exist together with fully developed broadcasting. In the long run the former are confined to functioning as mere distributors, and therefore potential importers of American products, while generalist television channels in industrialized countries are forced by the competitive logic of distinction and differentiation to strengthen their role as producers. American programmes thus tend to become a relatively smaller percentage in the large traditional networks of mature markets, while they can continue to grow in the ambit of narrowcasting. At the same time, American television drama is increasingly present in emerging markets such as Eastern Europe, which is now in a similar position to that of western countries during the 1980s.

The increase in the number of terrestrial and digital channels, as well as in transmission time – a channel that transmits continuously has to fill a little less than 9,000 hours in one year – inevitably leads to a massive recourse to foreign products, especially in a more or less protracted initial period. Over time, local products tend to replace imported products, and also tend to take over the most sought-after and competitive slots and those just preceding them (prime time and access prime time). Whether these changes are marginal or important enough to change the balance between foreign and local products depends on several specific circumstances: in particular the objective and subjective conditions of possibility and an economic, social and politico-cultural climate that favours a national television industry. Countries like Brazil and Australia have long since developed such an industry, and European countries are at various stages in the process.

We might object that national efforts of this type are relatively pointless, since satellite channels offer such a vast foreign selection, but there is another side to the story. Firstly, satellite channels and particularly pay-TV channels reach a relatively small audience even in the medium-term perspective of increased viewing. Secondly, national producers have an objective interest in entering the market and staying in it by offering a first-rate product and forming international alliances. Finally, the global channels and companies (CNN, MTV, Murdoch's News Corporation), which began by distributing only international programmes, are now developing their own programmes and offering products to various countries that contain substantial amounts of local content. This has proved that localization plays a crucial role in ensuring the success of satellite television.

Let us return meanwhile to the television programmes on offer today, in the form which they assumed and have on the whole maintained since the early 1980s. The overwhelming presence of American films and television drama is undeniable. Before we ask whether this is sufficient reason to declare the Americanization of national television schedules, especially those of Italy, a quick reminder may be useful as to why the need for content has been translated (in Italy, as elsewhere) into giving preference to the American supplier. In other words, what competitive advantage do American programmes have? At this point, I will simply list the practical market considerations and leave the cultural factors for a later discussion, although the two are obviously closely related.

The first reason why American programmes are prevalent lies in their price. In general it is easier and quicker to buy them than to produce an equivalent. They simply need to be purchased, dubbed and sometimes edited, whereas producing equivalent programmes is a long and complicated process. Above all, however, American programmes are particularly advantageous from the financial point of view. With a huge internal market of 250 million viewers and a lucrative secondary syndication market, production costs can be recovered (although this is becoming less and less the case) using domestic markets alone. Producers are then free to apply flexible pricing policies when offering their products abroad, depending on the purchasing power of the buyer; domestic production costs are higher, even for the most well-off. These prices in most cases are generally lower than cost of producing a similar programme locally, even for an important buyer. At the cost of a single hour of local production, the television channel can 'take home' or store many more hours of an almost ready-to-use American product.

Another reason for the success of American programmes is that they are serial *par excellence* (in all senses) and therefore available in large quantities. This is certainly a practical advantage in terms of decision-making. Buying the rights to an American series or serial guarantees that a large number of programming hours will be filled up in a single negotiation. This is a double guarantee, in that American television drama reaches the market only after it has satisfied the demanding rules of the most advanced industrial production and been tested on a very large audience. It has therefore gone through substantial testing and running in.

Finally, although European broadcasters have recently been making attempts at negotiating for single titles, many sales agreements include whole packages headed by a leading title. In this way, a desirable film or series drags along with it a large volume of hours, rather like the tail of a comet; for example, sitcoms, which once scheduled tend to increase the amount of American television drama on the air, even though no specific buying choice was made.

The fact that the American presence in this field is and continues to be predominant, in part for the reasons already suggested, does not equate to a complete Americanization of television. Television drama plays an important role, especially on private networks; but in Italy and most of Europe the largest percentage of television supply consists of locally produced programmes. Taken together, all the genres of television contents (news, entertainment, drama, sports, culture) remain predominantly national.

Furthermore, an American or other foreign programme is no longer exactly what it was when transmitted in its country of origin, once it is broadcast in a different context. Dubbing, advertisements and viewing time (Cohen and Roeh 1992; Ganz- Blättler 1997) are all gaps through which local elements infiltrate the international or global product, setting in train at the supply level – where the high rate of Americanization might seem indisputable – a process of domestication and indigenization.

4. Consumption: the tree hides the forest
It may indeed be true on the supply side that 'the media are American' (Tunstall 1977), but this assertion is subject to the distinctions mentioned above: not television in general, but television drama; not as a permanent state of affairs, but subject to variations in time and space. But on the consumption side things are different. It should be stated at once, as an introduction to the arguments that follow, that the extent of viewing of American programmes and their appeal to local viewers has been greatly exaggerated in public discussions and collective opinion. We do not need to espouse the theory that the public has become saturated with too much American television, although this may be true. We should rather uphold the structural nature of the gap between supply and demand for the foreign product, which has not come about by chance.

This statement may seem difficult to accept, since it is widely held that American television drama has a forceful impact and is irresistibly successful. This belief is by its nature contradictory, because it puts a premium on results (success, ability to please) yet underestimates the supposed reasons for these results, or explains them away as the seduction of simple-minded (if not vulgar) mass viewers by means of slick or escapist stories. It uncritically accepts the argument – though from a critical, that is to say, censorious perspective – that television gives the public what the public wants: an argument that can be either a justification or an accusation, depending on whether it is advanced by broadcasters or attributed to them. So if there is such a large supply of American programmes, one must deduce that they are requested and enjoyed in equal and ample measure.

Incontrovertible empirical evidence seems to bear out this conclusion, since a long list of successful American programmes comes easily to mind: from *Dallas* to *The Bold and the Beautiful*, from *ER* to *X Files*, from *Miami Vice* to *CSI*. In fact the source of the problem is that empirical data on viewers' choices are much less accessible to the public and much less transparent. It is easy to get a reliable picture of the programmes on offer through personal monitoring or just the experience of attentive viewers, or else by glancing through daily or weekly newspaper television pages, whereas only restricted groups of experts have access to systematic information about viewers' choices. Those doing genuine research in the field are confined to still smaller and more isolated groups of scholars and experts (we should point out that even academic research on international television flows tends to concentrate on the supply side).

People therefore tend to form their opinions about television consumption on the basis of personal preference, the preferences of family and friends, information about audience ratings and share (which is often misinterpreted), or undeniable evidence of popularity that is widely publicized in the media. These are all significant indicators, but they can often be idiosyncratic, selective, fragmentary and taken out of context. Any one or all of them risks creating the error of perception known as 'the tree which hides the forest' (De La Garde 1993); that is to say, a leafy and soaring canopy of the few successful programmes that conceals the thick undergrowth of less exalted offerings.

Metaphor apart, many American television fiction programmes were very popular in the 1980s in particular. Even today, American TV movies and series guarantee high ratings, depending on the different channels and time slots, or foster a fierce 'cultish' loyalty in more restricted audiences. But this success, or at any rate large public following, is limited to a few American imports; and no matter how many American programmes we might wish to add to the list, there will always be a limited selection of successes within an enormous supply, which consists mainly of products that never become popular or achieve cult status.

Despite this, local viewers habitually watch and enjoy American television fiction, especially when there is little home-grown television drama available, as used to be the case in Italy. Nor would I wish to suggest that the popularity of imported American programmes is a fabrication, or that it is based on insubstantial or second-rate products.

To recognize the presence of the forest and how far it extends behind the tree (going back to the earlier metaphor) means, however, that we must reject the idea of an automatic quantitative match between supply of programmes and audience viewing. Similarly we must reject the fanciful and phobic conception of American television drama as some sort of bewitching, flesh-eating siren or Pied Piper of Hamelin. If this conception were true, it would be impossible to explain either the modest popularity of many programmes (whether they are excellent or mediocre) or the fact that with a few rare exceptions, even the most popular American programmes never achieve the ratings and success of domestic drama. Although *ER* has a healthy following, it is no match for the enormous audience of *The Octopus* or *Marshall Rocca*, the hugely popular Italian television dramas. Even the home-grown Italian situation comedies, which have not yet entirely mastered the art, have a bigger audience than their often perfect American counterparts. Since the beginning of the 1990s an American television drama programme has on only one occasion enjoyed the following of an unusually large audience of over 10 million viewers; and that was for the opening episode of *Twin Peaks*, which then went on to lose a large percentage of its audience in the course of its run. The same thing has happened everywhere.

The truth is that the massive consumption of American television drama, far from being an established and irrefutable fact, needs to be reassessed, treated as an issue in itself and explained. Two interrelated concepts can help us here: cultural proximity and cultural discount.

Cultural proximity (Straubhar 1991, 1992) is a primary factor in orienting cultural demand and consumption, according to the need for and pleasure derived from recognition, familiarity and identity. Among the symbolic material that competes for the public's time and attention, people expect and are pleased to recognize themselves, their own social, individual and collective world, their customs and lifestyles, accents, faces, landscapes and everything else that they perceive as close and familiar. Since nothing is closer or more familiar than things that belong to or come from the society and culture to which people belong, audiences in a given country tend systematically to prefer and remain loyal to locally produced programmes *when they are available.*

The principle of cultural proximity – which usually takes precedence over, but by no means excludes, other criteria of choice – has been at work throughout the history of national television viewing. We see its interesting implications in the present era of satellite television. Here there has been a tendency (discussed above) towards localization of the contents that are broadcast by international channels, and the even more important phenomenon of large regional or geo-cultural markets (Sinclair, Jacka, Cunnungham 1996; Straubhaar 1996). In this context the term 'regions' means not only countries as geographic units, but also communities in various countries that share the same language, heritage and cultural affinity. The Hispanic language and culture, for example, bring together an enormous market stretching from Central and South America to communities and territories in the United States, Europe and Asia. (The community of Italian emigrants throughout the world, together with the population of Italy, make up a potential region of 120 million people). For the audiences of these regions, who have already brought about the creation of international television flow circuits that are no longer dominated by American products, satellite technologies are or can become the direct vehicle for programmes with a high degree of cultural proximity.

While this cultural proximity encourages the consumption of domestic products, cultural discount (Hoskin and Mirus 1988) reduces the consumption of foreign products. The two principles or criteria of choice in fact operate in the same direction. Since programmes rooted in a different culture lend themselves less well to activating mechanisms of recognition and identification, they are less attractive for a local audience: their value is reduced compared to local programmes. This reduction in value is the cultural discount.

It would obviously be one-sided and would require some sophisticated arguments to deny the popularity and international success of American programmes – success, that is to say, with viewers of different countries. The concepts of cultural proximity and cultural discount have not been introduced in order to deny, but rather to reposition, certain phenomena which despite seeming vast and uniformly widespread, are not in fact the norm and indeed in many respects fail to comply with the norm or infringe it. If the correlated ideas of cultural proximity and cultural discount normally serve to govern choice, how has it been possible for American programmes to take such an undeniably firm hold – though less than we would like to believe – on the viewing practices and preferences of such diverse local audiences?

The anticipatory socialization of Hollywood cinema must undoubtedly be seen as an essential pre-condition. American television programmes have enjoyed a minimal cultural discount in foreign markets, because the world where they originated was already familiar, thanks to films. But the most important reason for the success of American productions is to be found in their unique mixture of the particular and the universal, the local and the trans-national. Made for 'sophisticated and refined buyers' (Hoskins, Finn, McFadyen 1996), like the big networks, they catered in particular to the internal United States market and the largest possible national audience. The domestic US market is not only enormous, but is very much a mixture of different ethnic groups from different geographic areas and with different cultural heritages: a population essentially of immigrants. In order to speak to such a heterogeneous audience, held together though they may be by the myth of the melting pot, and in order to offer them multicultural materials and culturally appropriate programmes, it was necessary to develop a production capacity with a high degree of universalism; in other words, to pursue the 'lowest common denominator', as it is often scathingly called. The formulae, structures, themes, characters and values had to be accessible and recognizable to people from different cultures. All this has given American television drama a highly trans-cultural quality, and in consequence made it the unique example of a product whose particular local flavour rendered it an ideal export. The conditions of the internal market imposed specific requirements which turned out to be competitively advantageous in foreign markets. American programmes were conceived as popular stuff for a variegated local audience, indeed as popular national products for the most composite and multi-cultural of nations. This advantage was the key to their success as 'internationally-popular' products, to use the felicitous rewording of Gramsci's 'national-popular 'formulation, suggested by a Brazilian scholar (Ortiz 1988).

This is no longer entirely true, and has not been so for some time. Both American society and its televisual landscape have been subjected to disunity and fragmentation: these two things go together. The tendency towards 'neo-separatism' is widespread among ethnic and religious groups, males and females, members of different generations, new waves of immigration, especially Asians and Hispanics, as well as various movements and sentiments claiming the right to the unyielding pluralism of their own cultural identity. These movements accentuate social differentiation and segmentation and undermine the myth of the melting pot and of unity in diversity. Television broadcasting now brings together approximately a third of the general public; and the proliferation of cable and satellite narrowcasting channels addresses a growing number of restricted and focused audiences, made up of niches, targets and sub-cultures. Although they all purport to reach the largest possible audience in their own terms, the actual concept of the 'largest possible audience' has now changed, in both extent and internal composition. The ecumenical national audience of the past has broken up into the multiple audiences of the post-network era (Marc 1996; Curtin 1996; Newcomb 2002).

By going along with this tendency, American programmes run the risk of seeing the erosion of their universal quality and trans-cultural character which has minimized the cultural discount associated with foreign products, and has over time fostered their popularity (in every case, *after* the domestic product) with viewers in other countries.

5. Influences: the audience adopts and adapts

'They (the audience) first filter and reorganize whatever comes from the dominant culture and then they integrate it and mix it with the elements of their own historical memory' (Martin-Barbero 1993, p.74).

With a quotation that anticipates my conclusions I will introduce the final level of analysis, which is without any doubt the most problematic. What are the effects or influences of exposure to foreign, alien and exogenous cultural material? This level is extremely problematic, because the paradigms of cultural domination and colonization have, so to speak, built up their stronghold and constructed the hegemony of the theory of Americanization, automatically retranslating in terms of certain influences what was observable on the supply side and leaving out the intermediate stage of consumption. Here we can see effectively at work either the legitimate concern about the effects of the media (though here there is too often a tendency to evoke spectres or monsters) or the deeply rooted conception of a 'transmission' model of communication, that sees the public (specially, it would seem, those who watch television) as passive victims or 'cultural dopes', easily influenced by any or every programme or message.

A similar fragility is attributed to cultural identity. This is an elusive concept, but is called into play whenever there is a warning of the threat posed by global culture to the survival of local cultures.

Several factors serve to reinforce this concern, so often expressed in exaggerated rhetoric. First, there is the essentialist conception of culture or cultural identity; next, a vision of the horizons of everyday life that is too closely focused on the media (media-centrism). The essentialist idea, mentioned above, assumes as a given that local culture was originally uncontaminated, pure, and at the same time vulnerable. The 'media-centric' vision fails to recognize that in the rich network of situations and relationships which make up cultural experience, the media are only one element: an important one, but neither exclusive nor perhaps the most important. To return to imported American television fiction, a sense of proportion suggests that we should not exaggerate the impact of a single segment of the total amount of televisual material that is on offer.

It would clearly be too simple to invoke a sense of proportion. Whenever the discussion concerns cultural impact, it is useful to turn the question around and instead of asking, in this case, 'what effect does television or American television drama have on the audience?', ask instead, 'what effect does the audience have on American television drama?' Reformulating the question in this way, so that it considers the audience as an active 'doer', an agent, implies a theoretical reorientation towards the paradigm of an active audience. Indeed this theory is almost a truism in media studies (Morley 1992; Abercrombie and Longhurst 1998; Gauntlett and Hill 1999; Bechelloni and Buonanno 1999; Tulloch 2000), although in a range of meanings with various nuances.

To affirm that common discourse and opinion, in contrast to academic discourse, remain entrenched in regarding 'viewers as passive consumers' is perhaps not quite precise. What we observe rather is a polarization of positions, according to whether the speaker is considering himself or others. For no one doubts his or her own personal ability to control, monitor, and resist the fearful effects of media indoctrination, but we are not willing to recognize these qualities in the masses, who are presumed as a whole to be gullible. Yet this whole is a set of individuals, all of whom probably regard themselves as being aware of, and on guard against, the malign effects of television.

Then again, the point is not to avoid influences – everything, starting with chance, has an influence on our lives – nor is it to maintain the absurd thesis that watching American television drama leaves virtually no cultural trace. But this trace, however one may define it, does not necessarily equate to Americanization, that is to say the adoption and imitation of the models, values and lifestyles typical of American society and culture and the consequent destruction of local cultural identity.

Before they even become active, the viewers are situated in local cultures and so are anything but blank receptors. These are the very cultures that the paradigms of cultural domination are so worried about, yet without putting any trust in their capacity for resistance and renewal. In other words, it could be said that the audience is situated in different specific contexts, with different ways of thinking, acting and feeling, with different and equally specific resources, needs and problems. It is from these positions, based on and determined by nationality, class, education, gender, generation, and other elements, that the audience encounters and watches American programmes, among other cultural products.

To go back to where we started, what do viewers make of these programmes and how can this active model of consumption be explained? It is a work of interpretation, a hermeneutic process brought about by any communicative relationship, through which the fiction stories of American television acquire meaning, give pleasure, excite emotions, give rise to dreams and plans, and even provoke negative reactions such as conflicts and rejections: but all this happens within the frame of reference of locally situated life-worlds and contexts. Since the contexts are not homogeneous, the interpretation cannot be either. Nor indeed is the act of interpretation the mere decoding of prescriptive meanings, as was believed in the past. Rather it is the re-elaboration of cultural fragments, in this case foreign, which are recomposed and framed by the symbolic context of our own experiences and lives. If it is true that foreign products are adopted and incorporated in this way, it is still more true that this incorporation alters the original meanings and makes them different. Adoption always includes some form of re-adaptation, and consumption brings into play processes of transformation. The audience adopts and adapts (Smith 1992).

The corpus of empirical research where corroboration of the previous assertions can be found is perhaps somewhat limited (though one should bear in mind that the theory of Americanization is entirely speculative and conjectural), but it is significant. Recent studies of the reception of *Dynasty* in Norway (Gripsrud 1995), *Dallas* in the Netherlands (Ang 1985), Australia (Michaels 1988), Israel (Katz and Liebes 1990) and of *The Young and the Restless* in Trinidad (Miller 1992), and other studies (Biltereyst 1991) have all commented eloquently on not only the variety of responses to foreign programmes from different groups and subcultures, according to the viewing context, but also the invigorating effect that American programmes can have on local culture.

We encounter this last situation in the fascinating research of Daniel Miller, who learned of the success of the American soap opera *The Young and the Restless* while working on mass consumption and modern life on the island of Trinidad. Miller admits that he had not planned to study a soap opera, but was persuaded to do so by apparently fortuitous circumstances. At the time of day when the programme was broadcast, it was virtually impossible for him to do any field work because most of the local inhabitants were glued to their television screens. He later learned that the popularity of the programme with the islanders was closely tied to the idea of the 'bacchanal', a local term used to denote a mixture of scandal, gossip and disorder which the islanders consider the essence of their character and local traditions. In this American soap opera, so full of scandal, gossip and disorder, the Caribbean viewers found the anarchy of the bacchanal and recognized an important element of their own cultural identity. The pleasure they derived from this identification was all the greater, because local television programmes reflected the official culture and had few points of contact with popular traditions. So what to the conventional observer might erroneously be perceived as the consumption of a foreign cultural product that might tear people from their cultural roots, actually reinforced their ties to their own traditions. And although the environmental and social context of the product was a long way from the reality of the island, it was being reinterpreted and experienced as a true and lively expression of a local 'sense of place' (Buonanno 1997).

Miller himself admits that the example of Trinidad does not rule out the possibility that the viewing of American programmes might indeed in other places and at other times lead to the Americanization feared and proclaimed by cultural domination theories. It does, however, illustrate most eloquently that the cultural impact of these programmes is open to many different possibilities, and that the local act of viewing has the power, more often than one might think, to transform the content and meaning of the original foreign programme into a domestic version, in harmony with local historical memory and cultural tradition.

The creative, recombinant work of the processes of cultural indigenization is definitively put in motion within the wide range of empirically verifiable forms of the local adoption and adaptation of the programmes that are brought to viewers by international televisual flows. The consequences are diverse, but can not in any event be reduced to the monolithical unity of American domination.

7

TRAVELLING NARRATIVES

INTERNATIONAL FLOWS OF TELEVISION: FROM THREAT TO RESOURCE

1. Imagination and otherness

John Tomlinson's book on cultural imperialism (1991), to which I have referred in the previous chapter, opens with a picture in 'outdoor night' of an Australian family absorbed in watching television. Nothing out of the ordinary about that, comments the author, except that the scene has certain exotic features: the members of the (very large) family are aborigines, living in a semi-desert part of Australia, and the photograph was taken while they were gathered in a clearing in front of a humble dwelling, watching events on the glowing screen of a television set balanced precariously on a portable fridge at the edge of a small veranda. Tomlinson tells us that the original photograph was accompanied by captions that quoted *Dallas* and other western television programmes carried by satellite to the desert in the heart of Australia, and thus suggested that the scene should be read from the perspective of cultural imperialism: the uniqueness of an indigenous culture being put at risk by the domination exercised by technology, practices and content that were 'in a sense alien to their culture' (p. 2). From this point of view, it was clear that television, indeed the television set itself (and also perhaps the portable fridge), represented a 'cultural threat'.

Tomlinson, in the concept of cultural threat, crystallizes the obsession of the proponents of cultural or media imperialism with the danger of distorting or weakening native cultures through alien contact. This is the starting point of my discourse in this chapter. The term 'starting point' is very appropriate because in reconsidering international televisual flows (see chapter VI), I shall steer the argument in a more constructive direction as compared to the critique of the 'dominant paradigm' developed in previous pages: to this end I shall rely on the theories of travel and mobility. Along the way I shall turn the cultural threat into a potential resource and shall finally examine its unequal distribution and manifestation in the contemporary televisual landscape (in this way I shall salvage the media imperialism baby, who does not deserve to be thrown out with the all too abundant bath water).

I shall begin by taking my cue from the popular German saying quoted by Hulf Hannerz: 'Those who travel have stories to tell'[1] (2001, p. 142), in order to tell a travel story myself, by way of a prologue. I shall do this by deliberately imitating the beginning of a far more famous, resonant and influential travel story in the field of television studies: Raymond Williams' account of his first experience of American commercial television. He based his opportune, if controversial, concept of 'the flow' (see chapter II) on this experience, which was totally new to a viewer who had just arrived from the old continent. 'One night in Miami, still dazed from a week on an Atlantic liner, I began watching a film ...' (Williams 1992, p. 85).

Even though the flow of television as a sequence of uninterrupted programming, as Williams defines it, is different from the television flows that in this chapter coincide with the transfer of programmes in geographical space, the two different meanings of the term have a compatibility and a common foundation in the evocation of travel – in the first case, Williams' journey that originated the concept.

So I shall relate that 'one night in Bergen, bewildered by the persistent glare of the midnight sun, I began to watch television ...' For an inhabitant of Mediterranean Europe, even one who is accustomed to travelling around the Continent, Norwegian television in 2000 was probably no less alien than was American television, over thirty years ago, for a resident of the British Isles (with the addition of the language barrier). Switching quickly from one channel to another, I could not find anything that aroused not so much my curiosity and the stimulating sense of exploring something new and exotic (I was quite impervious to all this, being dazed by the lateness of the hour and the unaccustomed nocturnal glow) but rather any irresistible attraction to the reassuring and familiar. This was until my nervous and unsatisfying zapping from one channel to another came across the unmistakable figure of the detective Andy Sipowicz; and as I sat in front of *NYPD Blues*, I at last felt at home.

This type of experience is not at all exceptional nowadays. It may confirm the widespread belief that the main unifying factor of European television space consists in its American content; but it is of greater and more general interest if considered from the perspective of travel. In fact, we have here two dimensions of mobility that are interconnected and intersect each other: the physical mobility of the individual in real geographical space; and the transfer of cultural material in forms and symbolic meanings that are amalgamated into a narrative through international and intercontinental televisual flows.

This is how it happens that 'moving images meet de-territorialised viewers' (Appadurai 1996, p. 4). (It can happen in other ways: for example when a diasporic community is reached by satellite transmissions from their country of origin; Robins and Aksoy 2006). But even more important, the meeting of the two trajectories of de-territorialization can give rise to a re-territorialization (like feeling at home with *NYPD*) and to a new, if fleeting, and particular sense of place, where the latter is a 'textual place' and imagined (Tomlinson 1999). This 'sense of imagined place', an experience characteristic of mediatized society, is perhaps no less important for maintaining identity and the sense of ontological security (Giddens 1991; Silverstone 1994) than the sense of the real place, the result of first-hand experience and territorial knowledge.

Furthermore, the encounter between the mobility trajectories of individuals and symbolic materials comes about by exploring the screen, in actual fact a further form of travel. Televisual vocabulary relates to mobility and motion; we say 'stop here...stay here...go back', 'we walk, drive, fly, sail: we travel' (Larsen 1999, p. 114) on the television screen. Switching channels, especially in an environment reached by satellite television, often corresponds to a change in territory and therefore to the experience of a de-localization that takes on the meaning of an 'indirect or imaginary travel' (Urry 1995 and 2000). Peter Larsen cites the example of a Norwegian viewer who when interviewed in the course of research on cable television audiences, recapitulated her televisual experience the previous evening with the sentence 'I went to Sweden'. 'Obviously', the author comments, 'she is referring to what she did with the remote control, but she actually describes a movement in space...by her action she moved to another location' (Larsen 1999, p. 113).

'Television, more than any other technology, materializes the immemorial human fantasy of transcending the boundaries of time and space in a quest for another reality' (Loshitzky 1996, p. 324). The fact that television lends itself to being used as a sort of 'travel machine' (*ibid.*), a means not so much of transport in the true sense of the word but as a connection between different and distant spaces, constitutes knowledge embodied into our acquired experience, even though not all the implications of this have been grasped. We need not insist further on this point, except to recall that we do not necessarily perceive clearly, nor are we always aware of, what is part of our patrimony of experience. Not by chance are television viewers imagined more often as lazy and sedentary couch potatoes than as travellers in transit; and this very 'nomadism', easily recognized in present-day audiences, usually refers to a mobility that is entirely confined within the proliferating supply of channels and programmes, without being extended or related to possible movements within a space or imaginary shifts between territories.

There are two more associations, just as important for the discourse that I intend to develop, that are even less a part of the patrimony of a common reflective awareness. The first of these, which is actually the one I began with when quoting Ulf Hannerz (Walter Benjamin also quotes the same proverb, or a very similar one: 1966, p. 267) is between travelling and the work of the imagination. Travels generate stories: these are the inevitable and often quite felicitous products of the imagination, even when they claim to be faithful accounts; and the stories for their part make people travel in their imagination (and not only that).

Arjun Appadurai (1996) was the first contemporary scholar to give strong emphasis to the close and organic relationship between motion and imagination. Appadurai identifies the distinctive characteristic of modern subjectivity in the working of the imagination and, with an explicit reference to Durkheim, highlights its status as an authentic social fact of a public and collective nature. It is just as significant that he recognizes in the electronic media the primary forces that, together with migrations, powerfully fuel the work of the imagination in the present age. These propulsive forces mobilize, move and put into circulation both physical individuals and symbolic representations, and bring them together in sometimes unpredictable ways. Repertoires of possible lives and imagined worlds, outside the perimeters of local territories, present themselves to viewing or experimentation, to be imagined or lived by individuals, thanks to the images of the moving media and to real-life migratory movements. Media and migrations create the conditions of possibility for the construction of a 'plurality of imagined worlds', and offer new resources for it; these become part of the cultural experience of daily life. (An expression like 'plurality of imagined worlds' echoes social phenomenology in the words of Appadurai; see Berger, Berger and Kellner 1974.)

When brought to life by the electronic media, the workings of the imagination can become the driving force of individual and collective geographical relocations of a migratory nature. In this connection, Italian television's role in encouraging the migration of the thousands of young Albanians who disembarked on Italy's southern coasts in the 1990s is well known. As research has confirmed (Mai 2001), the Italian television programmes that were broadcast and gained widespread popularity in Albania after the fall of the Communist regime were able to offer mediated access to the tempting lifestyle of a glamorous and affluent Italy to a population that had been brought low by every sort of privation. This lifestyle would otherwise have been beyond the imagination of the Albanians; but once it had been revealed on their television screens and to some extent rendered tangible, it opened up horizons of what was possible, the imagination and hope of a different existence in a different country, and not infrequently persuaded people to act so as to fulfil this hope. Whether or not it was carried out, the migration project became an integral part of a new social subjectivity, 'a subjectivity that imagines different ways of being, different realities, diverse lives' (Mai 2001, p. 102).

Ethnographical research on a group of young South Korean working women (Kim 2005) tells us more about the 'imagination of freedom' and 'journeys of hope' that were inspired by the televisual experience. The interviewees lived with their parents, had no experience of tourism or living abroad and very little prospect of improving their own socio-economic status; watching western television programmes offered them the possibility of 'going' where they would never be able to travel. In gaining an idea of how people live in other parts of the world, the Korean women created points of reference for themselves in order to make up for the grey ordinariness of their daily lives by imagining new possibilities of social and geographical mobility. It was not simply a matter of escaping into a daydream, but of longing for the transformation and change that was generated and sustained by television. For these young Korean women, the author concludes, television had become an important resource for developing 'an imaginative social practice' (Kim 2005, p. 461) that allowed them to reflect on their own lives and to set off on a symbolic 'journey of hope' (Williams 1983, p. 268) that was not necessarily incapable of producing results in real life.

A further connection to be re-established is the relationship between mobility and the experience of 'otherness'. The same social phenomenology mentioned above provides some useful indications in this connection, so long as we are aware that in the phenomenological approach the pluralization of life-worlds means the extreme segmentation of the public and private spheres of modern society. We are in any case reminded that pluralization, entailing continuous relocation from one world to another (the word used Berger, Berger and Kellner is 'migration'), obliges individuals to become aware of the existence of 'others...[from this point to the end of the section the italics are mine] whose life is dominated by different, sometimes by contradictory meanings, values and beliefs' (p. 80).

The others, the strangers, the foreigners make up, so to speak, the raw material constituting the encounters that take place during travel and confer its power to transform. Eric Leed, one of the most distinguished contemporary scholars in this field, writes that ' travel in general is the channel where strangers appear in various forms and guises'[2] (1992, p. 25). People travel with ambivalent sentiments, since 'the joy of encountering diverse and strange realities'[3] (p. 95) is mixed with the anxiety and insecurity that are associated equally with what is different and strange and more generally unfamiliar to us. But those who are well-suited and accustomed to travelling tend to develop a habit of making comparisons: they compare the known with the unknown, ascertain the similarities and differences and end up by recognizing things as familiar that were previously strange and unknown.

I shall digress for a moment from the theme of travelling to introduce an annotation that may appear to be a diversion but is in fact relevant. Like travel, literature and narrative fiction may also be considered to be an opening to 'otherness': 'through literature we have the experience of the other and the others because we see the existence of so many possibilities, of different beliefs and conceptions of the world' (Turnaturi 2003, p. 43). We can easily see the relevance of this quotation if we recall that the images and sounds conveyed by international television flows, without being literature in the traditional sense of written narrative in the genre of the novel, have plenty to do with imaginative writing.

Encounters with 'the other' at different degrees of proximity are made possible and facilitated by indirect travel and symbolic and imaginary movements undertaken through the media, as well as, obviously, through physical relocation in geographical space by journeys in real life. Just as they can take the de-territorialized viewers back home, or to a familiar neighbourhood, the moving images are able to 'de-localize' audiences that are situated locally, introducing them to distant territories and the alterity of their inhabitants. James Lull (1995) remarks in this connection that we construct 'narratives of the *other*' (p. 149) through materials provided by the media. John Thompson (1995) emphasizes that 'individuals are able to gain some conception, however partial, of ways of life and life conditions which differs significantly from their own...' (p. 175), subsequently adding that 'the images of *other* ways of life constitute a resource for individuals (p. 176)'. For Arjan Appadurai the landscapes of technology and representation which he defines as 'mediascapes' offer the resources to create scripts of 'imagined lives, their own as well as those of *others* living in *other* places' (Appadurai 1996, p. 35).

Thus it happens that we come up against cultural 'otherness', the strangeness of strangers, in the travels of the imagination that are encouraged and multiplied by the electronic media. This may in effect mean thwarting the effectiveness of the precautionary measures that we take to distance ourselves, as soon as the strangers seem to have come straight into our home; yet it is precisely the mediated nature of the experience that creates a distance, that interposes a screen in every sense of the word, and keeps away the fear of the consequences of 'dangerous encounters', or encounters that are disagreeable or embarrassing, as we tend to think that encounters with 'cultural others' may turn out to be. According to Zygmunt Bauman, the televisual medium somehow produces a *cordon sanitaire* that in making us immune to risk also neutralizes our existential sensibility and our capacity for moral engagement. In the telematic city, or 'telecity' in the author's original definition, '... strangers may now be gazed at openly, without fear – much as lions in the zoo; all the chills and creeps of the roaring beast without the fangs ever coming anywhere near the skin... In the telecity, strangers are sanitised and safe, like sex with condoms' (Bauman 1993, p. 178).

Like John Tomlinson (1999) and Nick Stevenson (1995), I find the warning in Bauman's words somewhat disproportionate. Encountering 'otherness' without running risks or assuming commitments may indeed serve to make us indifferent or inattentive towards strangers of any origin or appearance; but the sense of shelter and immunity conferred by the mediation of the television screen can also enable us to look more carefully, with greater interest and even more benevolently, on the people and worlds of otherness.

2. Travelling narratives

I wanted to clarify my main interest in the capacity of the electronic media (a capacity that has not necessarily been exploited in their practical functioning, and which should not be regarded as the only one possible), and especially of television, to offer the public mediated access to territories that are far away from the context of their lived experience; to enrich their imagination of the 'other'; and thus to enable them to participate in inter-cultural encounters. I have done this through the concepts of de-territorialization, pluralization, imagination and otherness that I have already deployed, though more graphically than analytically.

In other parts of this book, especially in chapter V as far as televisual imagination is concerned, I have discussed at length the enormous expansion of the horizon of the mediated experiences in the world where we live. I have insisted enough on the need to consider this order of experience on the same level as a dimension of reality, phenomenologically diverse but not inauthentic or artificial compared with the reality of direct experiences. The latter may indeed take advantage of the irreplaceable prerogative of sensorial completeness and of the concrete nature of physical presence in a space-time conjunction; but mediated experiences reveal their capacity to widen and multiply, offering individuals symbolic access to innumerable representations of the possible. Thompson writes: 'The growing availability of mediated experiences thus creates new opportunities, new options and new areas for self-experimentation. An individual who reads a novel or watches a soap opera is not simply consuming a fantasy; he or she is exploring possibilities, imagining alternatives...' (Thompson 1995, p. 233). In many cases, one might add, the individual is experimenting in a mediated fashion and taking part symbolically in environments, social situations and aspects of existence that he or she would have little if any chance of encountering in real-life contact.

To claim that nothing similar has ever happened before the advent of the electronic media would be tantamount to historical amnesia. As we are reminded by Giddens, 'virtually all human experience is mediated' (1991, p. 23), if only through language and the spoken word. Over the centuries human beings have travelled in their imagination, listening to the stories and adventures of faraway regions that were told and sung by storytellers, bards and singers of ballads. Not by chance does Walter Benjamin identify the merchant sailor as one of the main traditional narrators: he travelled, or had travelled, and those listening to him would have shared his experiences of visiting other countries in an indirect or mediated way. While he was in prison, Marco Polo told Rustichello da Pisa about his journey to China. Even when Marco Polo's *Travels* were later available in print, the mass of people who could not read 'encountered' the Far East and its inhabitants through the oral descriptions of those who had read the book. In more recent times, the travel literature that has proliferated in books and magazines from the beginning of the nineteenth century has fulfilled the same function of 'placing distant and exotic regions within the national consciousness' (Lund 1993, p. 83).

So the phenomenon can hardly be considered new; but the modern media have intensified it through 'the tremendous increase in the mediation of experiences' (Giddens 1991, p. 24) that they brought about. Of course, there are many more forms of modern media than just television: films, newspapers, books, radio, cartoons, the Internet, each of them contributing in its own way to make us travel in our imagination and to bring awareness of other people living in other countries within our mental horizons.

Yet it is undeniable that television, among other modern media, has a special place and plays a prominent role. The television set is firmly established within the home; and most of our consciousness of the world is mediated by the small screen. The title of the well-known Australian soap opera *Home and Away* grasps and conveys the peculiar bi-locality of the televisual experience. More than any other, the domestic electronic medium enables us 'to be in a sense in two places at once' (Urry 2000, p. 67), potentially without any time limit, bringing into the home 'images of other places which provide a kind of imaginative travel which is complexly interwined with many processes of corporeal travel' (Urry 2000, p. 70). Thus, although television is an internal object that does not even requires us to move from the house, it is fundamentally *a medium of symbolic mobility*.

This argument is totally in accord with the position of those (including Massey 1994; Tomlinson 1999; Morley 2000 and 2001) who although they acknowledge the value of mobility as the central experience of the present-day condition, maintain that the metaphor of travel in the literal sense of people's physical relocation in a geographical space ought to be given less emphasis. It is a fact that most people have nomadic propensities to a greater or lesser degree; these are sometimes greatly romanticized and can equally be a privilege for fortunate people or a burden for marginal members of mankind. Doreen Massey, putting forward the influential concept of the 'geometry of power', has drawn attention to the unequal relationships that different people and social groups have with geographical mobility – not only in the sense that some of them regularly practise it (making a further distinction as to the scale of their travels, whether international, national or local) and others do not, but also in relation to the asymmetrical modalities of the link between the processes of territorial displacement and the capacity of those involved to exercise control over those processes. Some social groups, such as the international 'smart set', activate the processes, manage them with complete mastery and derive benefit from them; others, such as migrant labourers, endure them; still others, like people who live on the outskirts of cities, are imprisoned by them. The mobility experiences of a great many people, even today, are confined throughout their lives to little more than the daily journey between home and work.

'One rather direct way of posing the issue then', stipulates Tomlinson (1999, p. 151) 'is the distinction between literally travelling to distant places and "travelling" to them by talking on the telephone, typing at the computer keyboard or watching the television set'. The concept of travel must thus be preserved above all in its metaphorical meaning, so as to designate the twofold and often mutually articulated dislocation of firstly, cultural material (in the jargon of the television industry it is said, not by chance, that certain genres 'travel' and others do not) and secondly, human imagination. The electronic media are among the principal agents (thought not the only ones) of these forms and experiences of dislocation, equivalent to a journey without a departure, to a migration without leaving one's place of origin (S. Moores

2000). In their own way, they recognize and satisfy the universal right to depart and travel. Charles Baudelaire (quoted by Gitlin 2001, p. 55) once lamented: 'They left one right out of the Declaration of the Rights of Man and Citizen: the right to leave'.

My intention, at this point, is to reposition and re-examine the question, by no means resolved to date, of 'international television flows' from the theoretical perspective of travel. Even though I am aware that the various forms of mobility and the routes followed by television to other territories, especially in the conditions of growing inter-connection between contemporary television landscapes, cannot be fully described in the traditional terms of the 'flows' of television import and export, I maintain that the question continues to be very important, both theoretically and empirically – particularly insofar as the contents of the flows are the narratives and stories (in other words, television drama) that notoriously constitute the greater part of international television exchanges.

The anthropologist James Clifford (1997) coined the felicitous expression 'travelling cultures'. He wanted to put the emphasis on mobility, on the physical and symbolic movements through which cultures are created and recreated in the unceasing dynamics of inter-cultural import and export. He also recognized, in a conversation with Christina Turner, that the journey should not be understood in the referential sense. 'It's a mistake...to insist on literal "travel" ... It would be better to stress...that the travel, or displacement, can involve forces that pass powerfully *through*' (p. 28). The media, like tourists, commodities and armies, are powerful crossing forces, vectors of travelling cultures that in turn create the conditions for the symbolic experience of travel.

I will therefore introduce, following James Clifford, the definition of 'travelling narratives' to designate the fiction programmes that are involved in the import and export of television material. They are doubly connected to the theme of travel, both because they 'expatriate' from their places of origin and because, at their destinations, they are encountered by individuals who through them can achieve an experience of imaginary de-territorialization – the specific cultural experience of the mediatized world.

If the definition of 'travelling narratives' is appropriate for the current international flows of television drama, made up mainly of series and serials, this is also because it is confirmed by the story of serial narratives itself. In the course of the nineteenth century, American readers came into contact with serialized novels from the Old Continent (the forerunners of soaps and *telenovelas*), thanks to the transport by sea of books and other products from European publishing houses. Contemporary chronicles record that large groups of people would impatiently await the moment when transatlantic ships, having just moored in New York harbour, unloaded their cargo of *feuilletons* and serialized novels on the quayside. These took the form described by Giddens, quoting Susan Brooker-Gross, as a 'geographic bundling' (1991, p. 26). Since it was invented, that is to say nearly 200 years ago, fiction in serial form has gone back and forth between the continents, first migrating from Europe to America, then coming back into many European countries through the import of American and Latin American television series and serials.

International television flows ('travelling narratives' in my re-definition) can be seen in a new light in the context of this theoretical horizon. We may now be persuaded to consider these flows and re-conceptualize them as *flows of symbolic mobile and mobilizing resources* that have the potential to widen the range of our imaginary geography, multiply our symbolic life-worlds, familiarize ourselves with 'the other' and 'the distant' and construct 'a sense of imagined places': in short, to travel the world and encounter 'otherness' under the protection of the mediated experience.

3. The neutralized threat

We should naturally be aware that we are concerned with potential resources and that in this instance, as in many others, there is no purpose in being sentimental. Later in this chapter, I shall set out a position that will be a critique, not a celebration, of the empirical dynamics that still sustain international television flows today: in essence, what is travelling and in what direction, or which are the most travelled routes. For the moment I wish to emphasize the radical reversal brought about by the assumption of a 'resource' category, with regard to the theoretical approaches that have identified a cultural constraint or threat in the import and export of television programmes.

Some commentators have expressed serious alarm concerning the imminent danger of colonization and homogenization of indigenous cultures by foreign cultural material brought in by the media (in fact in most cases by American television programmes). This alarm emanates in particular from the perspective, well established for many years, of media imperialism. I do not need to recall the details of the widespread notoriety and influence of this concept, established as a genuine and dominating paradigm, having dealt with it extensively in the previous chapter. It is equally well known that the paradigm has been seriously and compellingly called into question for the past ten years, whether in its classic version or in its more recent metamorphosis into an integral variant, corollary or spin-off from the globalization theory. But although many arguments aimed at dampening down the alarm and lessening the risks have been convincingly deployed by numerous critics, and the exhortation to go 'beyond media imperialism' has been proclaimed more than once (Straubhaar 1991; Golding and Harris 1997), things have not progressed much towards a radical rethinking or the elaboration of an alternative to a theoretical construct that is based on the assumption of a cultural threat.

This assumption has however been deconstructed or invalidated by a vast amount of empirical literature (for example, Wang, Servaes, Goonasekera 2000; Elasmar 2003) and by an important work of discussion. From this work (and knowing that I run the risk of impoverishing the debate) I shall choose two of the conceptual categories that are most often and most authoritatively brought into the discussion.

The first concept is *hybridity* or *hybridization* (Garcia Canclini 1989; Pieterse 1995 and 2004; Kraidi 2002 and 2005), which is found in a vast range of more or less synonymous terms; 'mestizaje' (Martín Barbero 1993) creolization and syncretism (Hannerz 1996), indigenization (Appadurai 1996; Tomlinson 1999; Buonanno, above), glocalization (Robertson 1995). Hybridization, or any other term adopted to indicate the same thing – the processes of contamination and inter-cultural miscegenation – refers to a conception of culture as a symbolic and material complex that is 'in the making', in constant tension between permeability and resistance to the external influences that have to be faced with the passage of time. This is culture understood as a process or a flow, rather than as a permanent and uncontaminated structure.

'All cultures are the product of interaction, of exchanges, of influences coming in from elsewhere...' (Fabietti 1995, p. 21, quoted in Remotti 1996, p. 61) Probably no culture exists that has survived and developed without being modified and upset by its contacts and relations with alien forms and practices. What might appear at a quick glance to be an indigenous local specificity may turn out to be the result of a process of interpenetration in the medium and long term between the internal and the external. The music and the cuisine of many countries supplies the most obvious examples of this: one is reminded of the African and Latin American influences on American music, and of the many components of local gastronomy that originated from the productive inter-cultural encounters in cuisine (Morris 2002). From the point of view of hybridization, cultures – as has already been said about civilizations – assume the aspect of a patchwork quilt (Remotti 1996, p. 65).

Jan Nederveen Pieterse, a pioneer in the debate on globalization, observes with good reason how hybridity has rapidly become 'a routine, almost trite point of reference' in discourses on global culture; it is an attribute or a ubiquitous character that thus ends up by being 'meaningless, a universal soup: if everything is hybrid, what then does hybridity mean?' (Pieterse 2004, p. 108).

In reality the hybridity theories have the merit of countering what Pieterse himself defines as 'the fetishism of boundaries' – boundaries of culture, nation, language, civilization, religion and anything else – and above all of contributing fundamentally to *de-essentializing* the concept of culture and cultural identity as something pure and uncontaminated from the start, enclosed within an inviolable territory, and set in stone once and for all. What is in dispute is not the links between culture and territory, but what territory signifies: not a geographical space that is isolated within its own boundaries, but a piece of geography constructed from a history of material and symbolic relationships between the domestic and the extraneous, between identity and alterity. In substance, what is presumed in the discourse on media imperialism to constitute a perverse process in today's globalized world and a deadly threat to local cultures is converted in the theoretical perspective of hybridity into an ongoing historical process and a dynamic and vital potential for all cultures.

If we wish to respond to Pieterse's invitation and to theorize without sanctifying hybridity, we must acknowledge that this leaves several important questions unanswered. For example, there are different degrees and levels and stages of hybridization, and also varying measures of success or outcome (some hybrids undeniably do not succeed; there are cultural hybridizations that are infelicitous, riven by conflict, forced and a source of hardship and anomie). In the second and more importance instance, with which 'others', and in what terms of the reciprocal exchange, would there be the right conditions for hybridization? 'We are experiencing a "give and take" among cultures that encounter each other ... however nagging questions remain about who has given and taken what, what has been the result of such give and take...' (Wang and Yeh 2005, p. 177) Unresolved issues of power and symmetry of relationships are bound to emerge; we shall return to this point later.

The second conceptual category that has a strong impact in the critique of media imperialism is *cultural proximity* (Straubhaar 1991, 1992). We have already discussed in the previous chapter the workings of this 'compass', so to speak, which directs the first choice of viewers towards home-grown rather than foreign television programmes. Here it is worth adding the concept derived from John Galtung, with whom Joe Straubhaar, its proponent, originally associated it: 'asymmetrical interdependence'. Using Brazil and the Latin American countries in general as an empirical example, the author points out the role of cultural proximity in favouring the growing integration of the Spanish- and Portuguese-speaking markets. The emergence of powerful national television industries in countries such as Brazil and Mexico, heavily dependent in the past on the United States, has led to an export capacity within the regional area of Latin America; here Brazilian and Mexican programmes, or at any rate programmes originating within the same geo-linguistic region, compete effectively with American programmes thanks to their greater cultural affinity with local viewers. In numerous cases, Latin American productions have even reversed the one-way routes of televisual flows, reaching Latin-language viewers in Europe and North America. The earlier dependence is gradually evolving into interdependence, even if it is asymmetrical.

Hybridization and cultural proximity are powerful concepts: the two of them co-operate effectively in breaking up the alliance between 'the myth of uncontaminated culture' and 'the threat of imported media', as Nancy Morris (2002) recently defined the unproven assumptions that sustain so much of the writings on international television flows.

However, I believe that both hybridization and cultural proximity are concepts that are as intellectually illuminating as they are insidiously 'demobilizing' – if one accepts the reassurances they supply concerning the theoretical and empirical groundlessness of the cultural threat (homogenization, Americanization and so on): a threat that is inherent in internationally circulated television programmes, according to the writings referred to above.

We are now aware, in fact, that local cultures are not submerged in a global North American-style mélange, but blend creatively on contact with other cultures. We can see with our own eyes that however invasive the American or other foreign presence may be on national televisions, viewers will choose and prefer domestic products – and that viewers who are de-territorialized or who form a diaspora will do this by means of satellite technology, which has proved to be a purveyor of locality and not merely of globalism (Robins 1998).

I do not intend to belittle the importance of acquiring a more fine-tuned awareness of the dynamics of cultural change and of the preference models that orientate television viewing. I maintain rather that, having debunked the threat and discovered how to neutralize the risk, we should not delude ourselves into thinking that we have closed the books on the theories of international televisual flows. The fact that media imperialism and its associates have been consigned to the history, if not indeed to the archaeology, of television studies does not mean that all is going well

By what merely seems to be a paradox, it is the reversal of the first assumption – from the negative character of the threat to the positive character of the resource – that brings to light the critical situation that still persists in the field of the import and export of television drama. A reversal of this kind, inspired by the travel theories that we examined at the start, leads us to note a profound imbalance and a substantial deficit in the quantity and range of 'travelling narratives' on offer and accessible to a large proportion of present-day television audiences. I shall next consider the example of European countries, but the imbalance and the deficit to which they refer goes beyond the European case.

There is no need for us to abandon the context in which the effective debunking of media imperialism has been discussed in order to adopt this inverse perspective. The hybridization argument, in particular, integrates with it perfectly and provides appropriate starting points for problematization. Once it has been established that televisual imports are part of the perennial process of hybridization through which cultures come into being, develop and change, and that contact with 'cultural others' – here in the guise of foreign programmes – can therefore favour the formation of dynamic syncretisms, it clearly makes sense to ask ourselves which 'cultural others' we are given concrete possibilities for encounters, and perhaps for creative blendings.

Reformulated in the terms of my discourse, the question becomes: what is the provenance of the travelling narratives that are part of the choice offered to television audiences, even if they are less appealing than the home-grown programmes? To which territories do they give mediated and imaginary access? The answers to the question may vary in the details, according to the diverse geo-cultural areas of the world, but the model that they present is widely shared. It is a model in which the diversity of foreign television drama's origins boils down to just one source: generally, once again, the United States.

In drawing attention to the profound asymmetries of international relations in the sphere of the media, connected as they are to the imbalances of power in distribution of cultural materials, media imperialism has addressed a real problem. I will draw once again on John Tomlinson (1991) in order to make the point more clearly. Tomlinson, in discussing a case that is well known in anthropological writings – a researcher who happens to end up in a remote part of north-eastern Brazil and finds a group of peasants who seem to be enormously enjoying a Charlie Chaplin film on television – wonders whether it would be appropriate to invoke the universalism of Charlot, as others have done. This universalism is the capacity of an artist to touch the hearts of a group of people in such a way as to transcend divisions of class, nationality and culture. He wonders furthermore whether to invoke in the first instance the power of Hollywood to distribute its own pictures everywhere. 'One major reason why Chaplin's humour can be plausibly be seen as universal is that it is universally *present*' (p. 53), the author concludes.

Whichever way you look at it, this state of affairs remains a problem. This is not because of the old story of the cultural threat hovering above the head of indigenous cultures, but rather because the consequence will be a clear impoverishment of the symbolic resources that are available and usable for the experiences of de-territorialization, the work of the imagination, encounters with the 'plural other' and not least the actual processes of cultural hybridization.

4. The case of Europe
I should now like to bring my discourse back from the rarified zones of abstract theory to the solid ground of empirical reality. To this end I shall use the European television space as a quick case study, with particular reference to the supply of television drama in the five largest countries (Germany, the United Kingdom, France, Italy and Spain).

Periodical gathering of data (De Bens and de Smaele 2001) and longitudinal studies (Buonanno 1997–2006) show how a supply model for the scheduling of terrestrial television drama took shape in the main European countries during the 1990s, that could be roughly summarized in the dichotomy: prime time is domestic, off-prime time is American. This division between two different time bands (the short but valued evening slot on the one hand, the whole of the rest of the day on the other) serves to reveal the bi-polar structure of the supply: it is composed essentially of local television drama and American television drama. This dual hegemony leaves very limited margins for drama programmes from third countries, such as other European ones, Latin American, Canadian or Australian – which together, apart from some variation between different countries, have a share of no more than one-sixth of the total.

Although half to two-thirds of television drama broadcast in an average week in the five major European countries comes from the United States, it would be wrong to conclude that there is an immutable supremacy of the North American product over the domestic one. In fact the proportion of imports from the United States has been decreasing over the years: the historical series of the sample weeks monitored by *Eurofiction* records a fall from 65 per cent in 1996 to 49 per cent in 2005 (Buonanno 1997–2006), taking all five countries into account. Furthermore, in each European country the massive recourse to American products is confined to certain specific channels, more often than not commercial, which are characterized either by a target audience of young people or by the shortage of resources for original productions, or by an editorial policy that is biased towards a combination of qualitative and cosmopolitan criteria. In the United Kingdom, for example, a cultured minority channel like Channel 4 distinguishes itself by its selective supply of the best American productions.

Furthermore, an over-abundant proportion of American television programmes broadcast during the day is made up of repeats, whose temporal stratifications go back over decades. In addition, American imports have only limited access to prime time; and in general to time slots corresponding to the largest audiences. The programming strategies of broadcasters, supported by European and national regulations in favour of domestic production, co-operate to ration and marginalize imports. Take the case of the Latin American *telenovelas*: their presence outside Iberian television has been greatly reduced.

By contrast, it is the domestic programmes that take the lion's share during prime time. Thanks to the advantage of this position, they are the most watched and the most popular among national audiences, as of course happens in every part of the world (a repeated amount of striking empirical evidence confirms this). Viewers everywhere prefer their domestic programmes, which have the competitive advantage of cultural proximity. The convincing demonstration of the success of local television drama encourages broadcasters to increase production and supply (to the extent permitted by available resources); this is one of the factors that has contributed to the re-launching of national television industries over the last decade, particularly in Italy.

The opposing dynamics of expansion and contraction that affect respectively domestic and North American television drama do not impair but rather reinforce the bi-polar supply structure. Non-local and non-American programmes account for a brief appendage, which has remained in an inelastic fashion below the low threshold mentioned above.

A mapping of television drama programming in the contemporary television landscape thus reveals the existence of three areas that are unequal by reason of their range and importance:

- the area of 'cultural proximity': occupied by home-grown television drama, it has a limited but growing presence in the supply field, while it enjoys front-rank importance in the politics of programming and in viewing habits;
- the area of 'familiarized alterity', or 'domesticated otherness': in this zone, widespread but diminishing, we find the American programmes occupying a secondary position in programming schedules as well as in the models of audience preference;
- the area of 'marginalized alterity' or, properly, symbolically nullified otherness: this is where the remaining programmes are located. In this last narrow tract of territory, coinciding with the most marginal time slots, we find non-national European television drama and little else.

As far as the residual presence of programmes of European origin is concerned, we can put forward at least two plausible explanations. The first is an explanation based on industrial and commercial factors. According to these, the scarce circulation of national European programmes is attributable to a lack or insufficiency of a number of prerequisites: ample catalogues, formats and standardized languages and, not least, the capacity and indeed the will on the part of television producers and distributors to compete in international markets. The second explanation is based on cultural factors, and in this instance what is held responsible is not the lack but on the contrary the excess of requisites: namely cultural specificity, localism and the unmistakable and indispensable domestic flavour, all of which make television drama as attractive for its local viewers as it is unappreciated by viewers in other countries, who in turn are entrenched in their own linguistic and cultural specificities. That the English do not laugh at the same jokes as the Italians (or a similar assertion) is a truism that is much used as a definitive argument in discussions on the subject.

In fact the undeniable existence of industrial and cultural obstacles to the inter-European circulation of national television programmes obscures the fact that although production in each of the large European countries is still in large measure local and adjusted to the needs of its own public, it now includes an appreciable quantity of television drama that is suitable for export – also as a consequence of the processes of convergence in the evolution of formats and genres. Suffice it to say that German series have a wide circulation and enjoy a fair measure of success, benefiting not only from their greater resemblance to American products and from their specialization in the detective and adventure genre, but also particularly from the credit and recognizability that they have acquired thanks to the lead-in programmes or 'Trojan horses'. The detective series *Derrick*, for example, proved to be a powerful lead-in for the export of German television drama to many countries of Europe, because it met the trade prerequisites of a drama series available in ample quantity and the cultural prerequisites of a product that converted the stereotype of the threatening and ruthless German, stamped on the collective imagination by Nazism and the Second World War and reinforced by countless films on that era, into the reassuring and trustworthy figure of a dedicated (and almost always unarmed) upholder of the law. From the perspective of the provenance of the travelling narrative, this draws our attention to the important cultural role that can be assumed and carried out by exported television drama: it can help to model and re-model the image of the originating country, its character and lifestyle, that prevails in the receiving country. The German example cogently demonstrates how 'cultural discount' – the devaluation and in the worst case the loss of attraction and interest that home-grown products suffer when transferred to other cultures (see the previous chapter) – can be considerably reduced and converted into a measure of 'familiarization'.

In the case of Europe it is thus evident that a state of affairs resulting from circumstances, policies and practices that are now fixed but not set in stone has been *essentialized* and transformed into a sort of 'ontology', which expresses itself in a widespread and unquestioned conviction that 'European television drama does not travel well', especially in Europe. We note here that cultural proximity is a principle of preference, not exclusion (otherwise cultural behaviour and consumption that inclines towards the foreign and exotic would be inexplicable). Yet this widespread and unquestioned conviction is an example of how invoking the barriers of cultural proximity can result in rationalizing or rather naturalizing a state of affairs, that is in fact responsible for regenerating and perpetuating the very conditions it is presumed to spring from.

On the contrary, it is true that the binary structure of the supply, based on models of viewer preference as much as it contributes to supporting and reproducing these models, creates the conditions for an inhospitable environment for foreign programmes – even if they originate in neighbouring countries and have membership of the European Union in common. Obviously North American television drama is also foreign: but this is a *familiarized* foreignness; viewers have long been accustomed to watching such programmes, if only as a second choice.

The truth is that essentialistic conceptions, no matter whether or not they are consciously held, prevent us from seeing how the structures of collective feelings such as proximity and familiarity are built up, reconfirmed and preserved through their constant repetition. Proximity exists because it is reaffirmed; familiarity exists because we are regularly made familiar with it. In the same way otherness, distance and extraneousness are reconfirmed through marginalization and rejection.

Although discovering the new can give as much pleasure, each in its own way, as recognition of the familiar (Livingstone 1999) – the pleasure of travelling, never quite devoid of a measure of anxiety and uncertainty, rests in encountering new and different experiences – it is the renewal and legitimization of the near and familiar in present-day European television that wins in the end over new discoveries and familiarization with extraneous matters.

Cultural proximity, the distributive power of the American industry, the programming models based on minimizing risk and the claim to be 'giving the public what it wants': all these work towards diminishing, if not neutralizing, a primary resource of mediated knowledge and travelling narratives: access to the other than oneself, the experience of imaginary travel in territories elsewhere. The limited trans-national circulation of television drama produced in different European countries, for example, prevents televisual narratives from making an important contribution to the work of the imagination on the 'European other' and on the non-American 'other' in general. It is not a matter, in the European context, of cultivating the illusion of a common European identity. Philip Schlesinger (1991, 1993) has convincingly warned us in this connection against the rough determinism of the 'distribution fallacy': distributing the same cultural products does not lead to the same interpretations, nor to a common culture. It is enough to invoke the more modest objective of supporting an opening towards a 'plural other', though this will not necessarily produce a communal feeling or a shared culture.

It can be said definitively that cultural proximity can become a constraint, and that identity can assume the weight of a burden. It may be true that television has always been mainly involved in the national dimension, but this has not happened without awkward repercussions. James Curran (1998, 2002) has spoken of a syndrome of 'national distortion' in television, mentioning the insubstantial interchange of programmes between European countries as a case in point. Michael Tracey has directed his criticism towards the parochial nature that television is assuming and towards the 'domestic populism' that informs local products (1995). Kevin Roberts (1998) has warned us about the risk of creating cultural ghettos and has noted that the mere juxtaposition of diversity (parallel and mutually exclusive media communities) is not enough: there is a need for cultural encounters between diverse subjects and groups, so as to reconvert multi-culturality into inter-culturality.

In conclusion I should like to make it clear that what I regard as a serious problem is neither the centrality of domestic television drama in the panorama of televisual supply (viewers unquestionably need, like and have a right to watch programmes about their own country), nor the presence of the North American product (which is often of excellent quality and not infrequently more innovative and advanced than the domestic product). The problem to be resolved is rather the absence or the marginality of all the rest.

As I have tried to demonstrate throughout this chapter, the question of international televisual flows has until now been confronted in a spirit of fear and paranoia of the other, from an *anti* perspective – anti-American for the most part, but also anti-Japanese and anti-Latin American, according to whoever was 'the other', perceived as an invasive threat in the circumstances at the time. This might be the right moment to re-angle our perspective. Now that we are to some extent reassured by our discovery of the strength and resistance of local cultures, we should relocate our confidence and our suspiciousness – and perhaps be more suspicious of proximity and in any event more confident of alterity. We should affirm the value of encounters with cultural extraneousness at both the theoretical and the empirical level.

An American cop show, a Brazilian *telenovela*, a German action series, a Spanish comedy, an Italian melodrama, an English literary adaptation, or indeed anything else: travelling narratives from all parts of the world, coming together in a variegated televisual environment, receptive towards diversity, could contribute towards spreading 'an awareness of the world as a one of *many* cultural others' (Tomlinson 1999, p. 195).

It is true that they could more modestly be confined to constituting a 'global hotchpotch' of narratives, not unlike the disorderly gastronomic eclecticism that is one the most common manifestations of modern 'banal cosmopolitanism', according to Ulrich Beck's definition (2003, pp 205–206), reminiscent of Michael Billig's 'banal nationalism' (1995). In fact there is no guarantee that an experiential horizon crossed by 'travelling narratives coming from anywhere' will inspire a thoughtful awareness of cultural difference. But at the theoretical level it is a hypothesis that we must not exclude; and, at the empirical level, 'it does at least seem a disposition to be built upon that is plausibly within our grasp' (Tomlinson 1999, p. 207).

There may be something disorderly in this perspective. Why not? It is like the disorderliness of a fair, as we can imagine or experience it. For Michail Bakhtin (1981) the fair is closely linked to hybridity, since it is a place where one encounters the familiar and the strange, the resident and the foreigner; and the itinerant storytellers who used to roam around at the fair were the real-life raconteurs of the past travelling narratives, from which television drama is directly descended.

Notes

1. Translated from Italian: 'Chi viaggia ha delle storie da raccontare' (translator's note).
2. Translated from Italian: 'Il viaggio in generale...è il canale della comparsa di estranei in varie forme e sembianze' (translator's note).
3. Translated from Italian: 'La gioia dell'incontro con realtà diverse e strane' (translator's note).

STOPPING TIME
LIFE STRATEGIES IN THE FORMULAE OF TELEVISION SERIES AND SERIALS

1. The elemental structures of seriality

At the end of a book in which I have repeatedly articulated the theme of transformation of the experience of place, I shall now try to address an interpretative hypothesis concerning the televisual experience of time. In the field of television studies, dealing with the relationship between the electronic medium and the time dimension has meant in most cases referring to the immediate present of distant events, which viewers are enabled to attend at the same time as they are taking place. In substance it is the experience of 'liveness' (see chapter III in this connection).

I will now take my cue from 'liveness' and welcome the unusual and perceptive meaning put forward by Paddy Scannell: '"Liveness" refers when all is said and done to being alive, to the survival of our being. It is an existential phenomenon (the condition of our being)... [which corresponds] to the unique capacity of twentieth-century electronic technology to give us constant daily access, in unprecedented measure, to the life and times of the world in which we live' (2004, p. 141).

Life or 'life strategies', to use the words of Zygmunt Bauman (1992), are at the centre of this closing chapter, which once again draws on the inexhaustible range of reflections aroused by television narratives in order to bring to light the life-giving potential of their specific serial formulae. If we leave out all the intermediate stages for the moment, the interpretative hypothesis advanced in the next few pages could be summarized – though not simplified – in the following terms. The temporality of serial narratives is the building material for the 'processed and artificed thoughts' (Bauman 1992, p. 15), the elaborate subterfuges through which human cultures, and in this specific case the popular cultures of the modern world, keep anxiety about death at bay.

I must also warn the reader that for a good part of my discourse it will appear that I am not talking about television; I shall in fact be considering nineteenth-century narrative inventions, the process of secularization after the Enlightenment, even the *Arabian Nights*, and more still.

But this *tour d'horizon* is essential to enable us to arrive at the final contribution, as rich in meaning as it is unsuspected or unappreciated, made by television to the imagined experience of a crucial existential dimension.

It is necessary in any case to start with televisual seriality. Although it was not invented by television (as we shall see later) or used exclusively by television, narrative seriality has established an indissoluble link with the small screen and has become a defining factor of its identity. Televisual storytelling is serial *par excellence* and television is unquestionably the stronghold of narrative seriality in today's world.

It is not only the place where seriality features most frequently, feeding the insatiable hunger for televisual content with its capacity for textual proliferation, and even increasing the 'infinite diversity' (Barthes 1996, p. 46) of narrative genres; it is also and above all the place where narrative seriality assumes regular temporal structures that are not seen anywhere else in the same unique combination.

We learn from studies of time that the temporal regularity of every event or situation is organized according to a number of basic parameters or dimensions: their sequential structure (the order in which events take place), the duration (how long they last), their temporal location (when they take place), their rate of recurrence (how often they take place) (Zerubavel 1981, especially p. 1). Each dimension can assume characteristics that are more or less rigid or flexible and can produce various gradations of temporal regularity. Seen through these parameters, serial television fiction reveals a very high degree of regularity: this is expressed by the orderly and irreversible sequence of the episodes of the serial, and in large measure of the contemporary series; by the standardized length of the narrative segments (half an hour for the soap and the sitcom, one hour for the series, one and a half hours for the miniseries); by the preciseness and uniformity of the temporal collocations (in times of day and fixed days of the week); by the rhythmic cadences of their recurrences and intervals (every weekday for the soaps, once a week for the series).

It is true that the same structures of regularity operate for all, or nearly all, the contents and genres of television; and that at least two dimensions of temporal regularity – succession and periodicity – have always characterized the serial narratives of past and present. But by reason of being incorporated into television, narrative seriality comes up against a temporal regularization that is unprecedented and without equal.

I shall not labour this point further, except to emphasize how it helps to make serial television fiction a system that is highly predictable and thus dependable and reassuring. Dependability and reassurance are the prerogatives of the system, even before the models of plot development and the convention of the happy ending, and represent a resource that has important cognitive and emotional implications. As we are reminded by psychological and sociological theory, we need backgrounds or frameworks that are orderly, solid and secure: things that we can take for granted, to give complete sense to every segment and experience of everyday life. We need these backgrounds not only to receive confirmation but also to experience surprise, which being a reaction to the unexpected presupposes the existence of hopes and expectations.

The well-regulated temporal structuring of television fiction supplies precisely that orderly, solid and secure background on which the serial formulae display or 'speak' their *own* temporality and offer it for the construction of 'a fictive temporal experience'[1] (Ricoeur 1985, p. 105).

The narratives of the world are numberless, to express it in the manner of Roland Barthes (1996, p. 46). Nevertheless the enormous range and variety of televisual stories can be traced back, on the level of formal structures, to a *binary typology* of narrative formulae: the same formulae that one finds in any serial corpus since their origins in the nineteenth century, which up till now have not belied the tendency of popular fiction to establish a 'community of profound structures' across the heterogeneity of media and genres (Besson 2004).

This binary typology is composed of the *serial* and the *series*, which I define – deliberately echoing Lévi-Strauss – as the *elemental structures of seriality*. All television drama (with a few exceptions) can be traced back to two basic narrative formulae, characterized by the twofold properties of extension and reduction: they function in fact either as indefatigable multipliers of the narrative corpus, through the repeated generation of episodes and instalments, or as reducers of its enormous expansion, which in short finds itself facing the principles of order and the regulation of just two, or two pre-eminent, formal structures (though these are open to historical and geo-cultural variants, and to the frequent practices of reciprocal contamination and hybridization: Buonanno 2002).

Each of the two elemental serial structures is characterized by its own temporality, perhaps rather its own *temporal regime*, modelled respectively on an equally binary typology of the conceptions of time: linear and cyclical, or evolutionary and repetitive, modern and traditional or mythical. In particular, and quickly noted:

a. The *serial*, the direct heir of the nineteenth-century *feuilleton* (see below), is present in televisual narrative in the respective Euro-American and Latin American variants of the soap opera (open serial) and the *telenovela* (closed serial). It is characterized by a textual corpus divided into unfinished segments, set out in accordance with a rigid sequential structure (the first and the subsequent). Each narrative segment occupies a precise position in the temporal sequence of the story and is directly linked with what goes before and what follows. The chronological continuity of the serial inscribes the formula in the linear and evolutionary conception of time (the so-called 'time's arrow'), which in turn makes the world it portrays evolutionary and metamorphic.
b. The *series* similarly finds its origins in the tradition of nineteenth-century novels (see below), based on the formula of the independent and cumulative adventures of recurring heroes. Its organizational principle, unlike the serial, is based on autonomous and conclusive segments, self-contained in the narrative sense and thus not linked to a sequential structure (although the present-day tendency to contamination makes that principle a regularity but not a rule in the strict sense). The formula is a-chronological, instituting a regime of cyclical temporality: the world thus represented is in consequence an iterative world, preserved (relatively) from the metamorphic effect of time.

We shall see how the elemental structures of seriality put the temporality that informs them at the service of the inextinguishable human desire for immortality. A further dimension must be brought into consideration in this connection: the duration or, in the literal sense (sanctioned by dictionaries), the capacity to last in time. Translated into a textual extension that is sometimes immense (the soaps that go on for several decades) and always substantial (the hundreds of instalments of a *telenovela*, the hundreds of episodes of a multi-seasonal series), the *long duration* is a constituent property of seriality and forms a part, with differences of degree but not of substance, of the formulae as much of the serial (evolutionary duration) as the series (iterative duration).

2. Going back to the origins of the formulae

I have referred more than once to the nineteenth century, and with good reason. It is in this century, characterized as noted by Peter Brooks by an 'unquenchable thirst for plots' (1984, p. 5), that the switch to serials in the narrative structures of the West has occurred. We cannot plausibly maintain that seriality, in the sense of the existence of formulaic narrative structures, was born then; popular storytelling has always been in some ways formulaic and serial, and Greek tragedy itself can be traced back to the principles of seriality. Nevertheless, it was not till the nineteenth century that the specific elemental structures of seriality, the serial and the series, took shape and developed and, not least, attracted massive popularity. The coming into existence of prime historical conditions of a market for mass production and consumption of fiction, often used as an explanation for this – just as the advantages of industrial production and audience-chasing on the part of broadcasters are being invoked in the case of television seriality – certainly constituted a necessary condition; whether it was also a sufficient condition is quite another matter.

It is of course true that the *feuilleton* – to mention the most famous if not the only nineteenth-century serial 'invention' (Olivier-Martin 1980; Bianchini 1988): one should add the novels in instalments, the series of novels and the cycle of novels (Besson 2004) – was born for the purpose, which it fulfilled perfectly, of extending and consolidating the readership of the first mass-circulation newspapers. This does not explain why the *feuilleton* constituted a significant turning point and had a considerable impact, still perceptible today, on the history of narrative structure in the West. In order to account for the success of the *feuilleton*, it is necessary first of all to take into consideration the specificity of its formula.

I do not intend, from a formalistic abstract perspective, to disregard the fact that the fortunes of the *feuilleton* were in large measure to be ascribed to its contents, or to the type of stories being told: robust, melodramatic, highly imaginative and at the same time rooted in the social climate of the time, or preferably in its darkest and murkiest recesses, the depths of perversion, the intrigues of power and the hovels of destitution. I consider rather, in agreement with Hayden White (1987) among others, that the form is also rich in significant content and shall for this reason try to draw out and interpret this content.

The foremost of the strong points in the feuilleton's form was without any doubt the strategic device that produced narrative segmentation: the regular, systematic and institutional interruption of the story and the consequent suspension of the reading process. In this way, for the first time, a relationship was built up between text and reader based respectively on the promise and the expectations of the interruption. This was a firm relationship and destined to remain so, although it was built upon a taking away or withholding of pleasure – the pleasure of continuing to read – which appeared all the more frustrating by the fact that the interruption occurred at the most agonisingly interesting moment: the suspense at the end of the instalment.

In fact the strategic interruption (Iser 1978), which is the true original invention of the *feuilleton* and still remains the organizational principle of television serials, betrays an intuition that is broadly confirmed by modern theories of literature: the intervals between the reading (or the viewing) of a narrative, are not pauses or rests: they are spaces in the working of the imagination. In these liminal spaces, trapped between what we have already learned from a story and what we are still to learn, the imagination overloads itself with expectations and reaches out towards the new discoveries that will follow with the resumption of the narrative flow. An active involvement in the plot wells up in the mind of the reader, and a pleasure that intensifies the normal pleasure of the story, adding the thrilling tension of waiting for it to start again.

In systematically producing the conditions of imaginative overload for its readers by means of regular interruptions in the flow of the narrative, the *feuilleton* created a new modality of involvement and pleasure: or in other words it sensed and explored the generative capacity of involvement and pleasure that is inherent in the postponement of gratification. The suspension of the narrative in fact constitutes a postponement, a temporal delay, a means of deferring the satisfaction of the desire to know more and to listen to the rest; in the *feuilleton* this satisfaction was sometimes postponed 'until the last instalment', just as in a soap or a *telenovela*. But the deferral of satisfaction, which gives us time to anticipate it and to have a taste of it in advance, is in turn a source of pleasure and the *feuilleton* exploited it in full measure.

The second strong point of the *feuilleton* format – the lengthy duration of the storytelling, bearing in mind that novels in instalments lasted for months and months – hinged basically on the same principle of deferral: what was postponed and delayed was in this instance the conclusion of the story, the narrative closure. The fact that, as we know, it was above all the demands of the market that required the stories to be dragged out at great length – dragging out the subscriptions to the daily papers in the process – in no way undermines the clever game that the *feuilleton* instituted and maintained with the ambivalence of readers' wishes.

'Desire is the wish for the end, for fulfilment, but fulfilment must be delayed' (Brooks 1984, p. 111). In the circumstances of everyday life, just as in the specific experience of enjoying a narrative text, everybody experiences on numerous occasions ambivalent surges of yearning, like Zerlina's 'I would and yet I would not' in *Don Giovanni*. We are capable of thinking, at the same time, about a story that enthrals us that we cannot wait to know how it will end, and yet we would like it never to end. The plots of *feuilletons* aroused in their readers the desire to know how they would end, but this desire was not satisfied until the end of a long journey – and not even a direct one, punctuated as it was with interruptions, digressions and distractions. The delay of closure, in the *feuilleton*, coexisted with a format constructed on the dialectical tension between desire/pleasure of knowledge of the ending and desire/pleasure of the postponement of that same knowledge. Not by chance did it happen that when a story was particularly successful, the authors were implored to delay the ending. This shows how the demand for postponement, the 'permanent deferral and evasion of the problem of the end' (Brooks 1984, p. 110) got the better of the demand for gratification. The *feuilleton* satisfied the desire for postponement, extending the 'delaying space' of the story.

The novel with the 'recurring hero', progenitor of the modern television series, worked in a different fashion, drawing up a pact with its readers based on the promise and expectation not of interruptions and postponements but of a repeated satisfaction of the desire/pleasure of knowing the ending. Each narrative segment of the series of novels was a volume containing a complete adventure of the hero – a detective like Edgar Allan Poe's Auguste Dupin or Arthur Conan Doyle's Sherlock Holmes, a major criminal like Fantomas, and later Arsenio Lupin and Rocambole. In consequence the authors were not begged to delay the conclusion of the story, but to keep the characters alive and write more and more stories about them.

It is important to note how in series of novels, based on 'repetitive return' and not on evolution as in the *feuilleton* or the cycle (Besson 2004, pp. 22–23), the chronology was from the start only that of the publication of the volumes; in no case was it a diegetic inter-volume chronology. The characters and the setting of the story reappeared from time to time – as happens equally in present-day series, televisual or otherwise – without bringing any trace of the passage of time, and therefore placed in a non-temporal dimension that in effect made them timeless. These characters, and their readers with them, could allow themselves purely and simply to be unaware of time. Even before they gave life to true immortals, as was to happen later in comic strips, it became clear that series of novels aimed to defy death when Conan Doyle – under pressure from his readers – 'resuscitated' Sherlock Holmes, after having tried to get rid of him forever by making him fall down the Reichenbach Falls after being grabbed by his arch-enemy Moriarty.

We can see therefore that the two deep-rooted structures of modern popular fiction are made up by acknowledging and satisfying desires that pull readers in two different directions: on the one hand the protraction of the *same* story, a device adopted by the *feuilleton* and the novel in instalments; on the other hand the start of a *new* story, a task assumed by series of novels.

There is no contradiction, still less opposition, between the two formulae; if anything there is a sort of 'division of labour', a sharing-out of the tasks of satisfying narrative pleasures; and the effectiveness of this is borne out by the phenomenon of the extraordinary popularity – in truth with greater intensity in the case of novels in instalments – enjoyed everywhere, in France, England and the United States, by the new formulae (and, let it be understood, by the stories that were told in this way). We could (but would be only partially right) explain this away as enthusiasm for the latest fashion, if after nearly two centuries we were not in a good position to know that narrative seriality has long outlived its novelty phase and has put down deep roots.

There is furthermore no contradiction but rather a concordance between the two formulae, since in both cases we are in the presence of narrative structures that engage in a challenge to time, if for no other reason (but there are others) than to ensure for themselves, or more precisely for the stories that they fashion, a long life: the many months of a novel in instalments, the span over many years of a series of novels. This long life finds a parallel in the lifespan of its readers and thus comes to take shape as an 'institution' of seriality from the point of view of both production and supply and of consumption.

In both cases, the serial formulae – by means of the postponement devices of the *feuilleton* and the multiplying devices of the series of novels –assuage in the field of popular literature the inextinguishable 'thirst for a story' that dominated reading habits throughout the nineteenth century.

3. The theatre of immortality

If the nineteenth century thirsted after stories, this was perhaps because it thirsted after *sense*.

Walter Benjamin, Roland Barthes, Peter Brooks and Paul Ricoeur have all said inspired and enlightening things about the close connection between narrative and the processes of sense-making, in particular concerning the significance of the temporal experience. To the authors I have mentioned should be added the eminent cognitive psychologist Jerome Bruner, a convinced and convincing champion of the irreplaceability of narrative as a primary form for rationalizing the human experience (see chapter V). Bruner states (referring to all types of narrative from the literary novel to the anecdotes that we all tell, if only to embellish everyday conversation) that had storytelling not offered the possibility of framing an intelligible representation of world experience, 'we would be lost in a murk of chaotic experience and probably would not have survived as a species' (Bruner 1990, p. 56).

But now, making what may appear to be a sudden change of storyline whereas I am in fact following a logical train of thought, I shall refer to sociologists such as Bauman and Elias and historians such as Ariès and Vovelle, in order to draw on an authoritative (if limited) corpus of studies of death. The possibility of tracking down and establishing a nexus between the cultural attitudes of modern western society towards death and narrative seriality, is at the centre of my hypothesis. The fact that the nineteenth century was the cradle of both could be explained away as a coincidence, not as a connection. I believe that there are valid arguments for converting the former into the latter, trusting in the fact that 'popular and/or dominant narratives convey as a rule more information about the mentality and concerns of the socio-cultural setting in which they had been conceived and circulated than about their declared objects' (Bauman 1992, p. 148).

In his admirable study entitled *The loneliness of the dying* (1985), Norbert Elias lucidly states that the true problem of death – the problem of the finiteness of an individual life – rests not in death itself but in the awareness that one must die: a burden of awareness that human beings are the only living creatures to bear. 'Human beings know, and so for them death becomes a problem' (p. 5).[2] A burden of this sort has never been so heavy as it is for individuals today. Elias offers us a powerful and moving contemplation of the lonely state of the person who is dying: this lonely state is a consequence of the repression and concealment that contemporary society imposes on anything to do with death, in its efforts to keep away the unbearable thought of the 'extreme threat'. Similarly Antony Giddens (1991) includes death among the experiences that have been institutionally 'sequestered' from modern life; and Geoffrey Gorer has spoken of the 'taboo' surrounding death, which he alleges has replaced the taboo attached to pornography, in a famous article published in the mid-50s (1955).

It was not ever thus. The historian Philippe Ariès, who carried out important and weighty studies of the subject, coined the well-known definition 'tamed death' to describe the relationship with death – not only familiar but also in some measure serene and peaceful – that individuals maintained in pre-modern society. 'The old attitude in which death was both familiar and near, evoking no great fear or awe, offers too marked a contrast to ours, where death is so frightful that we dare not utter its name. This is why I have called this household sort of death "tamed death"' (Ariès 1974, pp. 13–14).[3] According to Ariès, it was only between the end of the eighteenth century and the beginning of the nineteenth that death, imbued with a sense of profound tragedy, started to cause fear.

The image of tamed death has in truth turned out to be as evocative as it is controversial, although even those who have welcomed it with critical caution – one of these being Norbert Elias himself – acknowledge that it is appropriate to suggest the idea of a relationship with a more intimate and everyday death, less encumbered and repressed than it was to become later. Yet this was no less fearful a relationship. One need only think of the iconographic tradition of the *danse macabre* to perceive the terror aroused by death well before modern times.

In fact the important question is not the terror of death, which pertained in all probability to every stage of human history, but the way in which human civilizations have worked through it and have tried to exorcise it over the centuries.

Echoing Elias, Zygmunt Bauman writes that 'human beings are the only creatures who not only know, but also know that they know – and cannot "unknow" their knowledge. In particular, they cannot "unknow" the knowledge of their own mortality"' (1992, p. 3). The 'anti-mnemonic tool' of our culture serves to keep this painful awareness under control; the enormous and successful effort of culture to give meaning to human life cannot bear fruit unless it is sustained by the equally enormous effort to forget the transience of our existence. Hence the unceasing creation of 'life strategies', the ingenious expedients, the elaborate subterfuges to deny the existence of death, or to delude oneself that one can keep it at bay by living as if it were of no concern to us.

Religion's promise of the soul's immortality has for centuries been one of the stratagems, probably indeed the most effective stratagem, a true antidote to death, converted from the departure from earthly life to the entrance to an immortal afterlife.

The advent of modernity, which certainly did not happen overnight but so to speak burst upon the latter half of the eighteenth century at the time of the Enlightenment, created the conditions for a radical change in the rules of the game. Society in the late eighteenth and the nineteenth century was bowled over by the processes of individualization and secularization and by the claim that Reason imposed its own supremacy; it lost faith in transcendence and shrank from religion's discourses on salvation and providence. 'The end of the hegemonic position and indeed the quasi-monopoly that Christianity has enjoyed concerning the final journey'[4, 5] (Vovelle 1993, p. 474) is one of the characteristic traits of this period of history.

From being tamed, if it ever was, death became 'wild'; from being an entry into another phase of existence, it became a mere exit. Above all, in a world where humans were for the first time enabled as individuals to mould their own life and where they felt the 'pressing need' to give sense to their life, it happened that death emerged as the only aspect of the human condition that could oppose an immoveable resistance to an effort of this kind. Human mortality was revealed to modern gaze as a failure of reason, a denial of every plan for supremacy over Nature and Fate, a complete affront to mankind.

It is not surprising that the nineteenth century, as is revealed to us by Michel Vovelle's masterly historical fresco, was a century obsessed with death in its philosophical musings just as in its artistic manifestations; nor that people should have been terrified and fascinated by it in equal measure, since their obsessions often assumed ambivalent forms. The entire Romantic movement stems from the fascination with death, as the classical work of Mario Praz (1988) has demonstrated once and for all.

At the same time, the nineteenth century firmly held the reins of a theme that was inherited from the century of the Enlightenment, a century that had already adopted it and above all given it philosophical and scientific legitimacy: the struggle against death. Such an expression (or however one might phrase it), such a concept is the most eloquent indication of the radical break with the pre-modern world which, without the need to be at peace with death, certainly did not conceive (and could not have conceived) the possibility of confronting it and thus opposing the Divine Will.

The rise in popularity of the vampire figure (resurrected from the folklore of Eastern Europe) and Mary Shelley's creation of Frankenstein may have absorbed from the *Zeitgeist*, and attest in the realm of the imagination, the hitherto unknown purpose of opposing human mortality. Similarly, in a province of the imagination that is no less prone to myth-making, the new figure of the investigator (the recurring hero, the serial hero, let it not be forgotten) is not unrelated to that purpose '...The new paladin... is the hero of the crime novel. Parsifal puts on Sherlock Holmes's clothes. He *hunts down death* (my italics), one blow after another'[6, 7] (Vovelle 1993, p. 586).

In the field of practical action and consequences, the struggle against death which –snatching the first decisive victories – the nineteenth century took upon itself, was conducted under the banner of an ideal consciously formulated in the late eighteenth century: the ideal of prolonging life and thus of postponing death (there is no other possible course, if one remains within the bounds of human capacity). The nineteenth century did indeed mark a change, of a general and continuous character, from the demographic models of pre-modern society: there was on the one hand a decline in famines and epidemics, those scourges that were responsible for sudden increases in traditional death rates, and on the other hand a rise, if an unequal one, in the living standards of the population (even though Engels and Dickens did not lie when they described the inhuman conditions suffered by factory workers); and above all, there was the therapeutic application of scientific discoveries in the field of medicine and related subjects. These were the main factors that allowed nineteenth-century society to experience the first victories over death in terms of a prolonging of human life, together with the first features of modernity.

Awareness of mortality naturally remains the burden that we know, never previously so oppressive. In turn, therefore, modernity formulated and put into action its own life strategies, its own 'ingenious techniques of exorcism'; now much more skewed in the direction of secular beliefs and practices. Bauman traces back the life strategies that accompanied the advent of the modern condition to two fundamental categories.

One of them is the *deconstruction of mortality*: once the impossibility of denying or eliminating death had been acknowledged, modernity created and continues to nourish hopes and expectations (as well as concrete conditions of possibility) of an almost unstoppable prolonging of life. By now it seems that one no longer dies of mortality and thus of an ineluctable component of the human condition, but of single specific and fortuitous causes – diseases, accidents, violence – that can be prevented, avoided or deferred. 'Doctors ... do not fight mortality; but they do fight ... each and any of its particular causes' (Bauman 1992, p. 139). Similarly the typically modern hubris that inspires this fight can at least celebrate its short-term triumphs over the surrogate targets of an unavoidable threat.

The other strategy, the *deconstruction of immortality,* consists for Bauman in making 'the whole of life into a game of bridge-crossing...so that no bridge seems to loom ominously like the "ultimate" one; none, most importantly, seems to be the bridge "of no return"... Nothing seems to vanish forever, for good, so that it cannot reappear again' (1992, p. 173). Although this is not one of the author's clearest formulations, and though elsewhere he seems to allude to a sort of round of ephemera with a post-modern stamp, one can pick up the unequivocal references to a repetitive circularity that aims to deny the irrevocable character of the points of no return.

We find again, in Bauman's interpretation, the motifs of deferral and starting again, the same motifs that, as we know, dominate the formulae of seriality; and we should not lose sight of the important signal of the secularization of the life strategies that have been constructed on the condition of modernity, nor forget that the advent of modernity coincided with the experience of the longest lifespan that humans have ever known.

Thirsting for sense, the nineteenth century sought it avidly in the secular instrument of the novel, which underwent an extraordinary flowering at both the cultured and the popular level: in some measure the triumph of imagination over reason. We are entitled to think that the strategies of exorcising death were in turn entrusted (together with much else, let it be understood) to the discourses of literature, both high and popular. Certainly, if novels have discharged the task of offering points of reference in a rapidly changing world and large and small subterfuges to defuse the anguish of finiteness, they have done it essentially through the stories they have told.

But it is not in fact implausible that popular fiction, by tradition formulaic, has invested these same formulae with an analogous task of making sense and exorcising the ending: those profound structures of seriality which, because of their capacity to perpetuate themselves, lend themselves well to being defined as 'survival formulae'.

4. The 'frame story' of the Arabian Nights
It is plausible, not least because there are precedents. Well before the nineteenth century, and outside the western world, the victory of narrative seriality over death had already found its own allegorical origin in the famous corpus of popular Indo-Persian stories: the *Arabian Nights* (AD 900–1100).

Bruno Bettelheim (1991), from whom I have taken the definition 'frame story', read it as a therapeutic work; Peter Brooks considers it to be a grand allegory of the driving force of narrative desire. But the *Arabian Nights* is more than that: it is a parable of the vital and life-giving force of serial fiction.

It will suffice just to recall the basis of the stories. King Shahryar, fuming with rage against the female sex after having discovered that his own wife had been unfaithful to him, asked his Vizier to bring him a young virgin every night, whom he would exploit sexually and then put to death that same night. Within three years there were no more girls in the country: they had all been put to death or had fled with their families. There remained only the two daughters of the Vizier, and the elder one Scheherazade – a young woman exceptionally learned in history and literature – offered herself as a sacrifice, but with a secret plan to avoid that fate. In the king's presence, she asked if she could bid farewell to her younger sister, with whom she had made a plan; and after the king had lain with Scheherazade, her sister asked her to tell a story to pass the rest of the night. The narration fascinated the king, who spared the girl's life; and this went on for a thousand and one nights, until Scheherazade, who meanwhile had had three children by the king, became his wife.

The stories that were told over the years, with regular instalments and suspense, night after night, one following closely on another, often organized in cycles and in anthologies (stories about birds, the voyages of Sindbad, the story of women's cunning), all of them told within the framework and against the background of the nocturnal meetings between Scheherazade and the king, vividly make up a serial narrative structure of masterly complexity, in which we recognize the forms and formulae of contemporary televisual seriality: the serialized series, the continuity and at the same time the daily interruption of the instalments of the serial, the anthological organization of the episodes.

Two specific points deserve greater attention. The first concerns the moment when the storytelling is interrupted. Those who have not read the *Arabian Nights*, or who read them a long time ago and have a hazy memory of the work, might think that Scheherazade ended each story at dawn and started a new one the next night. In fact our storyteller broke off in the middle of each story, to resume it and finish it the following night before starting a new one. Let us draw directly on the text describing the first night:

> At this point in her tale, Scheherazade saw the approach of morning and discreetly fell silent. Then her sister Dunyazad said: 'Sister, your words are sweet and gentle and pleasant to the taste'. And Scheherazade answered: 'Indeed they are nothing to that which I would tell both of you tomorrow night, if I were still alive and the King thought good to spare me.' On this the King said to himself: 'By Allah, I will not kill her until I have heard the rest of her tale' (1986, vol I, pp 12–13).

The interruption of the narration in the *Arabian Nights* does not coincide with the end of the story, with true narrative closure, but with a suspension of the act of storytelling; and this suspension, knowingly deployed by the expert narrator, is the hook on which Scheherazade ensnares the king's desire to hear 'the rest of her story'. The fascination exercised by the tale, a constant of human history, here has an intensifying mechanism in the interruption of the narration, in the *postponement of the ending* of the story, which reveals a new source of pleasure, heightening the tension of waiting.

In turn the suspension of the narrative – and this is my second important point – is also the suspension of the sentence or prospect of death. 'I swear that I will not put her to death until…'

the king promised himself; and Scheherazade knows well that the duration of the storytelling equates to the duration of her own life, and that she will remain alive just so long as she can sustain the wish of the king to 'hear the rest of her story'. From another point of view, the long drawn-out narration is destined to provide salvation for the king as well; as Bettelheim observes (1991), the king is a prey to emotional turmoil brought about by deep-seated inner grief, and Scheherazade's tales are his therapy. The depth of this grief is demonstrated by his need to listen to *countless* stories. Traditional Hindu medicine used to cure emotionally disturbed people with fables; the king needed a thousand fables, but after three years – during which he changes from being a provider of death to a creator of life, becoming the father of three children – he is cured.

The close connection between the stories and the storytelling with the time of life and death, the symbolic significance of the healing properties that are inherent in the *repeated* action of narrating, the narration of *long* stories and the *delayed ending* of the story take on maximum transparency in the *Arabian Nights*. All of the action takes place under the banner of a constant dialectic between the prospect of death, ever-present on the horizon of possibility – and present from the start in Scheherazade's awareness – and its repeated and finally definitive postponement.

5. The story is there, just like life

In concluding with the statement 'The story is there, just like life', the celebrated opening phrase of the introduction to his structural analysis of stories ('innumerable are the world's stories'), Roland Barthes aims to emphasize the universal character of storytelling 'present in every age, in every place, in every society...' (1996, p. 46). But one can legitimately ascribe a further significance to that proposition: that of a close correlation between the story and the course of life, a correlation made up of the joining together of a beginning, a middle and an end, to be found in stories as much as in human existence.

There is probably no need to cite theoreticians and narrative theories to support the idea, even intuitively, of the story as the metaphor of life. It is, however, appropriate to turn to authorial sources in order to draw from such an intuitive premise the conclusion that the ending, the narrative closure – the structural component and conclusion of every story, just as the closure of life is the conclusion to every existence – thus, corresponds to a 'death figure'. 'We need to think further about the deathlike ending, its relation to origin, and to initiatory desire', suggests Peter Brooks (1984, p. 96). Brooks, along with others including Paul Ricoeur who have addressed the issue, recalls Frank Kermode (1966), author of a study on the 'sense of an ending' that remains a point of reference forty years after its original publication. 'The great charm of books', states Kermode, 'is that they have an ending' (1966, p. 23). If narrative closure is a charm 'that cannot be denied' (p.23), it is because it supplies a point of view that embraces the whole of the story that has been told, and lets us see it as an intimately harmonious ensemble. We yearn for this coherence and harmony between the beginning, the development and the end of the story; and yet we fear the ending, because it is a symbolic representation of (our) death. The happy ending, suggests Kearney (2002, p. 160), is perhaps a consolation, a desirable and desired compensation for the loss of the story.

The solution offered by storytelling to the problem of the conflicting impulses between desire and fear, attraction towards/flight from/the final moment of the story, rests in the practice of introducing repetitions, digressions, changes of tack, fresh starts and delays within the delaying spaces of the story: a sort of safety distance, created and maintained through the deferral of the reconnection between the beginning and the end. Delay, postponement, deferral, but also repetition and fresh starts are moves and processes embedded in the temporal dimension. Furthermore, as has been recorded in a masterly fashion by Paul Ricoeur, the principle of make-believe deploys its own infinite resources in order to create 'imaginative variations on time'[8] (Ricoeur 1988, p. 127); or, in other words, to 'subvert or, perhaps better, pervert time: which is what narrative does' (Brooks 1984, p. 111).

The moment has come to turn finally to the narrative formulae of seriality that flourished in the nineteenth-century period of the popular novel, migrated successively through all the mass media, and matured and spread very widely through the elective encounter with television. The course followed by seriality up till now corroborates, in my opinion, the hypothesis that what I defined at the beginning as the elemental structures of televisual seriality (and fiction in general) make use of their own capacity to reconfigure time, in order to enact 'a permanent deferral and evasion of the problem of the end' (Brooks 1984, p. 110). These structures thus co-operate, each one according to its own *modus operandi*, with the 'anti-mnemonic working' of modern and contemporary culture in dealing with human awareness of death.

I shall now try to trace some concluding trains of thought.

Serial narrative had its origin in an historical phase during which, among other things, the attitudes of western culture towards death began to change. It was in the early decades of the nineteenth century, in the post-Enlightenment climate and coinciding with industrialization and modernization, that the first tendencies towards secularization emerged and the certainties and promises of salvation of the great religious narratives began to be eroded.

By now death was no longer, or was continually less, redeemed by the prospect of eternal salvation. It was from that point that death truly began to represent a problem and that the exorcising and the institutional 'sequestration' of death from everyday life became a distinctive trait of modern society. I think it is plausible to trace a connection between the two things – the birth of the serial narrative and the unbearable nature of the finiteness of life – and to hypothesize that the former played and still plays a part as one of the many symbolic and metaphorical devices that aim to exorcize our ending. Serial television narratives pursue and achieve a similar plan through the masterly means of temporal manipulation: extending time or stopping it.

What is revealed here is a utopian/subversive tension, but we could also agree with Bauman that it is a typically modern 'hubris' of the formulae, which we ought to consider as being one of the primary resources (though it is certainly not the only one) of the enduring attraction and fascination of serial narratives. This hubris rests in exercising a domination over time that allows the ending of the story to be delayed at will, even to the point of removing it from the horizon of possibility, or to be 'neutralized' by means of a repeated return to the beginning.

The *delay and removal* of the ending are the prerogative of the *serial*, which adopts the linear and evolutionary concept of time but manipulates it – in particular in the case of the open serial – by deferring or denying its irreversible progress towards a terminal point of no return.

The neutralization of the irrevocable sense of an ending is instead the prerogative of the *series*, which restores the mythical concept of cyclical time and – through the eternal return to the present – sets the suspension of time itself against its unstoppable flow.

The two great formulae of televisual seriality resort to different temporal subterfuges, but their opposed and complementary 'life strategies' operate by being driven by an identical ambitious project to fulfil our desire to master time: a chimera that never ceases to seduce us with its promise to remove the threat of the ending.

One of the main threads running through this book is the rich potential of 'the multiplying of experiences' that is inherent in television. The considerations addressed in this final chapter suggest an opportunity to integrate the framework, adding that the televisual medium – thanks to the unprecedented volume of serial narrative, structurally predisposed to the exercise of a twofold faculty for dominating time – 'multiplies the experiences of eternity', as Paul Ricoeur says of fictional narrative in general (1988).[9]

If such an assertion seems exaggerated, we can limit ourselves to turning round the banal accusation that is so often levelled at television – that it encourages viewers to escape from or avoid real life – and acknowledge that it displays, on the widest scale known in history, the characteristic that the great serial novelist J R R Tolkien (quoted in Kearney 2002, p. 160) ascribes to popular stories: that they offer a narrative solution to the dilemmas of time and the end and satisfy, with the breathtaking resources of the imagination, the ancient and profound human yearning to achieve the 'Great Flight' – not from life but from death.

Flight from death, survival, aliveness. If conceived, according to Scannell, as an existential phenomenon that 'refers when all is said and done to being alive, to the survival of our being' (Scannell 2004, p. 141), it is unquestionably true that, by expressing itself on an unprecedented scale and scope, 'liveness' confirms the unique and precious prerogative of the television experience.

Notes

1. French original text.
2. German original text.
3. German original text.
4. Translated from Italian: "La fine della posizione egemonica e anzi di quasi-monopolio di cui aveva goduto la religione cristiana per quanto concerne l'ultimo passaggio" (translator's note).
5. original text.
6. Translated from Italian: '...il nuovo paladino...è l'eroe del romanzo poliziesco. Parsifal veste i panni di Sherlock Holmes. Egli bracca la morte, un colpo dopo l'altro' (translator's note).
7. Translated from Italian: 'moltiplica le esperienze di eternità' (translator's note).
8. French original text.
9. French original text.

BIBLIOGRAPHY

Aarseth E., 2003: *We all want to change the world*, in Liestol G.., Morrison A., Rasmussen T. (eds.), *Digital media revisited*, The MIT Press, Cambridge, pp. 415–442.

Abercrombie N., 1996: *Television and society*, Polity Press, Cambridge.

Abercrombie N., Longhurst B., 1998: *Audiences*, Sage, London.

Allen R. C., Hill A., (eds.), 2004: *The television studies reader*, Routledge, London.

Altman R., 1986: *Television, sound*, in Modleski T. (ed.): *Studies in entertainment*, Indiana University Press, Bloomington, pp. 39–54.

Anderson B., 1991: *Imagined communities*, Verso, London.

Anderson C., 2005: *Flotsam*, "Flow", vol.2, n. 2, jot.communication.utexas.edu/flow/.?issue=2005/04/.

Ang I., 1985: *Watching Dallas*, Methuen, London.

Ang I. , 1966: *Living room wars*, Routledge, London.

Appadurai A., 1990: *Disjuncture and Difference in the Global Culture Economy*, in Featherstone M., *Global Culture*, Sage, London.

Appadurai, A., 1996: *Modernity at large*, University of Minnesota Press, Minneapolis.

Arabian Nights: *Book of the Thousand Nights and One Night*, Routledge & Kegan Paul, London 1986.

Ariès P., 1974: *Western Attitudes toward Death: From the Middle Ages to the Present*, Baltimore: Johns Hopkins University Press. Translated from *Studien zur Geschichte des Todes im Abendland*, Hanser, Munich, 1976.

Bachmair B., 1991: *From the motor-car to television*, 'Media, culture and society', vol 13, n. 4, pp. 521–533.

Bakhtin M., 1981: *The dialogic imagination*, University of Texas Press, Austin.

Banks A., Banks S.P., (eds), 1998: *Fiction and social research*, AltaMira Press, Walnut Creek.

Barthes R., 1996: 'Introduction to the structural analysis of narratives'. In S. Onega, & J. A. G. Landa (eds.), Narratology (pp. 45–60), Longman, New York.

Bauman Z., 1992: *Mortality, Immortality and Other Life Strategies*, Polity Press, Cambridge.

Bauman Z., 1993: *Postmodern ethics*, Blackwell Publishers, Oxford and New York.

Bauman Z., 2002: *Society under siege*, Polity Press, Cambridge.

Bechelloni G., 1984: *L'immaginario quotidiano*, ERI, Torino.

Bechelloni G., 1995: *Televisione come cultura*, Liguori, Napoli.

Bechelloni G., Buonanno M. (a cura di), 1999: *Audiences, multiple voices,* Edizioni Fondazione Hypercampo, Florence.

Beck U., 2003: *La società cosmopolita,* il Mulino, Bologna (no English version).

Benjamin, W., 1966: *Angelus novus,* Einaudi, Turin.

Berger P., Luckmann T., 1967: *The social construction of reality,* Anchor Books, New York. Peter Berger and Thomas Luckman. *The Social Construction of Reality: A Treatise in the Sociology of Knowledge.* Garden City, NY: Doubleday, 1966.

Berger, P., Berger, B., Kellner, H., 1974: *The homeless mind,* Vintage Books, New York.

Berger, P. L., Huntington, S. (eds.), 2002: *Many globalisations,* Oxford University Press, Oxford.

Besson A., 2004: *D'Asimov à Tolkien. Cycles and séries dans la literature de genre,* CNRS, Paris.

Bettelheim B., 1991: *The Uses of Enchantment: The Meaning and Importance of Fairy Tales,* Penguin Books, London.

Bianchini A., 1988: *La luce a gas e il feuilleton: due invenzioni dell'Ottocento,* Liguori, Naples.

Billig M., 1995: *Banal nationalism,* Sage, London.

Biltereyst D., 1991: *Resisting the American hegemony: a comparative analysis of the reception of domestic and US fiction,* 'European Journal of Communication', vol 6, n. 4, pp. 469–498.

Bourdon J., 2000: *Live television is still alive: on television as an unfulfilled promise,* 'Media culture and society', vol 22, n. 5, September 2000, pp 531–556.

Boyd-Barrett O., 1977: *Media imperialism. Toward an international framework for the analysis of media system,* in J. Curran, M. Gurevitch, J. Wollacott (eds.), *Mass communication and society,* Arnold, London, pp. 116–135.

Brooks P., 1984: *Reading for the Plot: Design and Intention in Narrative,* Clarendon Place, Oxford.

Bruner J., 1990: *Acts of meaning,* Harvard University Press, Cambridge.

Bruner J., 2002: *Making Stories,* New York: Farra, Straus and Giroux.

Buonanno M., 1996: *La piovra. La carriera politica di una fiction popolare,* Costa & Nolan, Genoa.

Buonanno M., 1997: *Il senso del luogo,* RAI-ERI, Rome.

Buonanno M., 1999: *Indigeni si diventa,* Sansoni, Milan.

Buonanno, M., 1999: *Faction,* Liguori, Naples.

Buonanno M., 2002: *Le formule del racconto televisivo,* Sansoni, Milan.

Buonanno M., 2004: *Realtà multiple. Concetti, generi, audiences della fiction tv,* Liguori, Naples.

Buonanno, M. (ed.), 1997–2006: *Eurofiction. Television fiction in Europe,* European Audiovisual Observatory, Strasbourg.

Caldwell J. T., 1995: *Televisuality. Style, crisis, and authority in American television,* Rutgers University Press, New Brunswick.

Caldwell J. T., 2000: *Theorizing the digital landrush,* in Caldwell (ed.), *Electronic media and technoculture,* Rutgers University Press, New Brunswick.

Canclini, N. G., 1989: *Culturas hibridas,* Editorial Grijalbo, Mexico City (Italian version: *Culture ibride,* Angelo Guerini Editore, Milan 1998).

Carey J., 1989: *Communication as culture,* Unwin Hyman, Boston.

Carey J., 1998: *Political ritual on television: episodes in the history of shame, degradation and excommunication,* in Liebes, T., and Curran, J. (eds.), *Media, ritual and identity,* Routledge, London.

Caughie J., 1990: *Playing at being American,* in P. Mellecamp (ed.), *The logic of television,* British Film Institute, London.

Clifford, J., 1997: *Routes*, Harvard University Press, Cambridge.

Cohen A., Roeh I., 1992: *When fiction and news cross over the border*, in Korzenny F., Ting-Toomey S. (eds.), *Mass Media Effects Across Cultures*, Sage, London.

Corner, J., 1997: *Television in theory*, 'Media, culture and society', vol. 19, no. 2, pp. 247–262.

Corner J., 1999: *Critical ideas in television studies*, Clarendon Press, Oxford.

Couldry N., 2002: *Media pilgrims. On the set of Coronation Street*, in Allen R. C. Allen, Hill A.(eds.): *The television studies reader*, Routledge, London, pp. 332–342.

Couldry N., 2003: *Media rituals. A critical approach*, Routledge, London.

Curran, J., 1998: *Crisis of public communication: a reappraisal*, in Liebes, T., and Curran, J. (eds.), *Media, ritual and identity*, Routledge, London.

Curran, J., 2002: *Media and power*, Routledge, London.

Curtin M., 1996: *On edge. Culture industries in the neo-network era*, in Ohmann R. (ed.), *Making and selling culture*, Wesleyan University Press, Hanover.

Dallamano P., 1956: *Il televisore*, in "Il Contemporaneo", no. 36.

Dayan D., Katz E., 1992: *Media events. The life broadcasting of history*, Harvard University Press, Cambridge. French edition *La télévision cérémonielle*, P.U.F., Paris 1996.

Dayan D., 1997a: *Media events*, in Horace Newcomb (ed.) *Encyclopedia of television*, http://www.Museum.tv/archives/etv/M/htm/M/mediaevents/mediaevents.htm.

Dayan D., 1997b: *La télévision cérémonielle*, seminar held on 14 May 1997 at CNRS, Paris, unpublished.

Dayan D., 2001: *The peculiar public of television*, 'Media culture and society', vol. 23, n.6, pp. 743–765.

De Benedetti A., 1953: *La televisione e i suoi fantasmi*, 'La nuova stampa,'30 October, p. 3.

De Bens E., e de Smaele H., 2001: *The inflow of American television fiction on European broadcasting channels revisited*, "European Journal of Communication", vol. 16, n. 1, pp. 51–76.

DeFleur M., Ball-Rokeach S., 1982: Theories of mass communication, Longman Higher Education, New York. (Italian version: *Teorie delle comunicazioni di massa*, Il Mulino, Bologna 1995).

De La Garde R., 1993: *Dare We Compare?*, in De La Garde, Gilsdorf, Wechselmann (eds.) *Small nations, big neighbour*, John Libbey, London.

De Rita L., 1964: *I contadini e la televisione*, il Mulino, Bologna.

Elasmar M. G. (ed.), 2003: *The impact of international television*, Laurence Erlbaum Associates, London.

Elias N., 2001: *The loneliness of the dying*, Continuum, New York 2001. Translated from Über die Einsamkeit der Sterbenden, Suhrkamp Verlag, Frankfurt-am-Main, 1982.

Ellis J., 1982: *Visible fiction*, Routledge and Kegan Paul, London.

Ellis J., 2000: *Seeing things*, I.B. Tauris Publishers, London.

Elsaesser T., 1988: *National cinema and international television*, in C. Schneider C., Wallis B. (eds.): *Global television*, Wedge Press, New York.

Fabietti U., 1995: *L'identità etnica. Storia e critica di un concetto equivoco*, La Nuova Italia Scientifica, Rome.

Ferguson M., 1992: *The mythology about globalization*, 'European Journal of Communication', 7, (1), pp. 69–93.

Feuer J., 1983: *The concept of live television. Ontology as ideology*, in Kaplan A. (ed.), *Regarding television*, American Film Institute, Los Angeles, pp. 12–21.

Fiske, J., Hartley, J., 1978: *Reading television*, Methuen, London.

Fiske J., 1987: *Television culture*, Methuen, London.

Fiske J., 1994: *Media matters: everyday culture and political change*, University of Minnesota Press, Minneapolis.

Galtung J., 1971: *A Structural theory of imperialism*, 'Journal of Peace Research', 2, pp. 81-117.

Ganz-Blättler U., 1997: *Series in Lynch. Language transfer as cultural transfer in european TV market*, in Bechelloni G., Buonanno M. (eds.): *Television Fiction and Identities*, Ipermedium, Naples.

Garelli F., 2003: *Il sentimento religioso in Italia*, "Il Mulino", n. 5, pp. 814-822.

Gauntlett D., Hill A., 1999: *TV living. Television, culture and everyday life,* British Film Institute, London.

Genette G., 1976: *Figure III. Discorso del racconto*, Einaudi, Turin.

Gershuny J., 1992: *Revolutionary technology and technological revolution*, in Silverstone R., Hirsch E. (eds.), *Consuming technologies*, Routledge, London.

Giddens A., 1991: *Modernity and Self-Identity*, Polity Press, London.

Giddens A., 1990: *The consequences of modernity*, Polity Press, Cambridge.

Giddens A.,1999: *Runaway world*, Profile Books Ltd, London.

Gitlin, T., 2001: *Media unlimited*, Henry Holt and Co., New York.

Goffman E., 1985: *Behaviour in public places*, The Free Press, London.

Golding P., Harris P. (eds.), 1997: *Beyond cultural imperialism*, Sage, London.

Goodwin P., 2004, *The UK from speculation to reality*, in Colombo F. (ed.): *TV and interactivity in Europe*, Vita e Pensiero, Milan.

Gorer G., 1955: *The pornography of death*, "Encounter", November 1955, then in *Death, grief and mourning in contemporary Britain*, Doubleday, London 1965.

Gripsrud J., 1995: *The Dynasty years*, Routledge, London.

Gripsrud J., 1998: *Television, broadcasting, Flow: key metaphors in tv theory*, in Geraghty C., Lusted D., (eds.), *The Television Studies Book*, Arnold, London.

Gwenllian –Jones S., Pearson R. (eds.), 2004: *Cult television*, University of Minnesota Press, Minneapolis.

Hall E., 1984: *The dance of life. The other dimension of time*, Anchor Books Editions, New York.

Hannerz U., 1990: *Cosmopolitans and locals in world culture,* in Featherstone M., *Global culture*, Sage, London.

Hannerz, H., 2001: *La diversità culturale*, Il Mulino, Bologna.

Hartley J., 1999: *Uses of television*, Routledge, London.

Heath S., 1990, *Representing television*, in Mellecamp P. (ed.),*The logic of television*, BFI Publishing, London, pp. 267-302.

Horton D., Wohl R., 1956: *Mass communication and para-social interaction: observations on intimacy at distance*, 'Psychiatry,'19, pp. 215-223.

Hoskin C., Mirus R., 1988: *Reasons for the US Dominance of the International trade in television programmes*, 'Media, culture and society', 10 (4), pp.499-515.

Hoskins C., Finn A., McFadyen S., 1996: *Television and film in a free international trade environment: US dominance and Canadian responses*, in McAnany E., Wilkinson K. (eds.): *Mass media and free trade*, Texas University Press, Austin.

Iosofidis P., Steemers J., 2005: *European television industries,* British Film Institute, London.

Iser W., 1978: *The Act of Reading*, Johns Hopkins University Press, Baltimore.

Jancovich, M., Lyons, J. (ed.) , 2003: *Quality Popular Television*, BFI, London.

Jedlowski P., 2000: *Storie comuni*, Bruno Mondadori, Milan.

Katz E., Liebes T., 1991: *The export of meanings: cross-cultural readings of Dallas*, Oxford University Press, Oxford.

Kearney R., 2002: *On stories*, Routledge, London.

Kermode F., 1966: *The sense of an ending*, Oxford University Press, Oxford.

Kim Y., 2005: *Experiencing globalization. Global TVv, reflexivity and the lives of young Korean women*, 'International Journal of Cultural Studies', vol. 8 (4), pp. 445–463.

Kompare D., 2005: *Rerun nation*, Routledge, London.

Kozloff S., 1992: *Narrative theory*, in R. C. Allen (ed.): *Channels of discourse, reassembled*, Routledge, London.

Kraidy, M. M., 2002: *Hybridity in cultural globalization*, 'Communication theory', vol. 12, pp. 316–339.

Kraidy M. M., 2005: *Hybridity. Or the cultural logic of globalization*, Temple University Press, Philadelphia.

Laing S., 1991: *Raymond Williams and the cultural analysis of television*, 'Media, culture and society', vol. 13, n, 2, pp. 153–169.

Larsen, P., 1999: *Imaginary spaces: television, technology and everyday consciousness*, in Gripsrud, J. (ed.), *Television and common knowledge*, Routledge, London.

Leed Eric J., 1991: *The mind of the traveller*, Basic Books, New York (Italian version: *La mente del viaggiatore*, Il Mulino, Bologna 1992).

Leed Eric J., 2006: *Shores of Discovery: How Expeditionaries Have Constructed the World*, Basic Books, New York (Italian version: *Per mare e per terra*, Il Mulino, Bologna 1996).

Livingstone S., 1999b: *What's new about new media?*, 'New media and society', no. 1 (1), April, pp. 59–66.

Livingstone, S., 1999a: *Mediated knowledge: recognition of the familiar, discovery of the new* in Gripsrud, J. (ed.), *Television and common knowledge*, Routledge, London.

Loshitzky, Y., 1996: *Travelling cultures/travelling television*, 'Screen', vol. 37, no. 4, pp. 323–335.

Lull J., 1990: *Inside family viewing*, Routledge, London.

Lull J., 1995: *Media, communication and culture. A global approach*, Columbia University Press, New York.

Lund, M., 1993: *America's continuing stories*, Wayne State University Press, Detroit.

Mai N., 2001: *Italy is beautiful. The role of Italian television in Albanian migration to Italy*, in King R., and Wood N. (eds.): *Media and migration. Construction of mobility and difference*, Routledge, London, pp. 95–109.

Marc D., 1996: *Demographic Vistas*, revised edition, University of Pennsylvania Press, Philadelphia.

Martín-Barbero, J., 1993: *Communication, culture and hegemony*, Sage, London.

Martín-Barbero, J., 2002: *Communicational hegemony and cultural dis-order*, in Bachmair B., Scalamonti A., Kress G. (eds.): *Media, culture, and social worlds*, Liguori, Naples.

Massey D., 1994: *Space, place and gender*, Polity Press, Cambridge.

Mattelard A., 1979: *Multinational corporations and the control of culture*, Humanities Press, Atlantic Highlands.

McCarthy A., 2001: *Ambient television*, Duke University Press, Durham .

McKee A., 2003: *What is television for?*, in Jancovich M., Lyons J., *Quality popular television*, British Film Institute, London.

Meyrowitz J., 1985: *No sense of place,* Oxford University Press, New York.

Meyrowitz J., 1993: *Images of media: hidden ferment - and harmony - in the field,* "Journal of communication", n. 3, pp. 55–66.

Meyrowitz J., 1998, *Multiple media literacies,* "Journal of communication", n. 1, pp. 96–108.

Michaels E., 1988: *Hollywood Iconography: a Warlpiri Reading",* in Drummond P., Paterson R. (eds.): *Television and its audience,* British Film Institute, London.

Miller D., 1992: *The young and restless in Trinidad: a case of the local and the global in mass consumption,* in Silverstone R., Hirsch H. (eds.): *Consuming Technologies,* Routledge, London, pp. 163–182.

Montalbetti C., 2001, *La fiction,* Flammarion, Paris.

Moores, S., 2000: *Media and everyday life in modern society,* Edinburgh University Press, Edinburgh.

Moores S., 2005: *Media/theory,* Routledge: London.

Morley D., 1986: *Family television. Cultural power and domestic leisure,* Routledge, London.

Morley D., 1992: *Television audiences and cultural studies,* Routledge, London.

Morley, D., 2000: *Home territories. Media, mobility and identity,* Routledge, London.

Morley D., 2001, *Belongings: place, space and identity in a mediated world,* "European Journal of Cultural Studies", vol. 4(4), pp. 425–448.

Morris, N., 2002: *The myth of an unadulterated culture meets the threat of imported media,* "Media, culture and society", vol. 24, pp.278–289.

Morse M., 1990: *An ontology of everyday distraction,* in Mellecamp P., *Logics of television,* British Film Institute, London, pp. 193–221.

Negroponte, N., 1995, *Being digital,* Alfred A. Knopf, New York.

Newcomb H., Hirsch P., 1987: *Tv as cultural forum,* in Newcomb H. (ed.): *Television, the critical view,* Oxford University Press, Oxford, pp. 455–470.

Newcomb H., (ed.), 1997: *Encyclopedia of television,* Fitzroy-Dearborn Pub., Chicago.

Newcomb H., 1999: *La televisione. Da forum a biblioteca,* Sansoni, Florence.

Newcomb H., 2002: *One hour of prime time. Television negotiations in the 50-Channel world,* in Bachmair B., Cavicchia A., Kress G. (eds.): *Media, culture and social worlds,* Liguori, Naples, pp. 139–155.

Nordenstreng K., Varis T., 1974: *Television traffic-A one-way street,* reports and papers on mass communication n. 70, Unesco, Paris.

Olivier-Martin Y., 1980: *Histoire du roman populaire en France,* Albin Michel, Paris.

Ortiz R., 1988: *A moderna tradição brasileira,* Editora Brasiliense, São Paolo.

Pasquier D., 1999: *La culture des sentiments. L'expérience télévisuelle des adolescents,* Editions de la Maison des Sciences de l'Homme, Paris.

Peters J. D., 1999: *Speaking into the air,* University of Chicago Press, Chicago.

Peters J. D., 2006: *Media as conversation, conversation as media,* in Curran J., Morley D. (eds.), *Media and cultural theory,* Routledge, London, pp. 115–126.

Pieterse, J. N., 1995: *Globalization as hybridization,* in Featherstone M., Lasch S., Robertson R. (eds.): *Global modernities,* Sage, London.

Pieterse J. N., 2004: *Globalization and culture. Global mélange,* Rowman and Littlefield Publishers Inc., Lanham.

Pickering M., 2001: Stereotyping: The Politics of Representation, Palgrave Macmillan, London.

Praz M., 1988: *La carne, la morte e il diavolo nella letteratura romantica,* RCS Sansoni Editore, Florence.

Press A., 1991: *Women watching television. Gender, class and generation in the American television experience*, University of Pennsylvania Press, Philadelphia.

Rajagopal A., 2001: *Politics after television*, Cambridge University Press, Cambridge.

Remotti, F., 1996: *Contro l'identità*, Laterza, Bari.

Richeri G., 2004: *The history of interactive TV*, in F. Colombo (ed.), *TV and interactivity in Europe*, Vita e Pensiero, Milan.

Ricoeur P., 1984: *Time and narrative* vol. I, University of Chicago Press, Chicago.

Ricoeur P., 1985: *Time and narrative* vol.II, University of Chicago Press, Chicago.

Ricoeur P., 1988: *Time and narrative* vol. III, University of Chicago Press, Chicago.

Ridell S., 1996: *Resistance through routines*, 'European Journal of Communication', vol. 11, no. 4, pp.557–582.

Robertson R., 1995: *Glocalization: time-space and homogeneity-heterogeneity,* in Featherstone M., Lash C., Robertson R. (eds.): *Global modernities,* Sage, London.

Robins, K. , 1998: *Spaces of global media*, www.transcomm.ox.ac.uk/.

Robins K., Aksoy A., 2006: *Trans-national media and migrants' minds*, in Curran J., Morley D. (eds.): *Media and cultural theory*, Routledge, London, pp. 86–99.

Rogers M., Epstein M., Reeves J., 2002: *The Sopranos and HBO brand equity. The art of commerce in the age of digital reproduction*, in Lavery D. (ed.), *This Thing of Ours. Investigating 'The Sopranos'*, Columbia University Press: New York, pp. 42–60.

Saraceno C., 2003: *Changes in Italian families from sixties to present*, in Del Boca D., Repetto-Alaia M. (eds.), *Women's work, the family and social policy*, Peter Lang, New York.

Scannell P., 1996: *Radio, television and modern times*, Blackwell Publishers, Cambridge.

Scannell P., 2004: *Broadcasting storiography and historicality*, "Screen", vol. 45, n. 2, pp. 130–141.

Schiller, H. I., 1969: *Mass communication and the American empire*, Augustus M. Kelley, New York.

Schiller, H. I., 1976, *Communication and cultural domination*, White Plains, New York.

Schiller, H. I., 1985: *Electronic information flow: new basis for global domination?,* in Drummond P., Paterson R., (eds.), *Television in transition*, BFI, London.

Schiller H., 1991: *Not yet the post-imperialist era*, 'Critical studies in mass communication', 8 (1), pp. 13–28.

Schlesinger, P., 1991: *Media, state, nation*, Sage, London.

Schlesinger, P., 1993: *Wishful thinking. Cultural politic, media and collective identities in Europe*, "Journal of Communication", vol. 43, pp. 6–17.

Schutz, A, 1964: Collected Papers, Vol III, Nijhoff, The Hague.

Schutz, A., 1970: *On Phenomenology and Social Relations*, University of Chicago Press, Chicago.

Schutz A., 1974: *The Stratification of Life-World*, in Schutz e Luckmann, *The Structures of the Life-World*, Heinemann, London.

Schutz, A., Luckmann T., 1974: *The structures of the life-worlds*, Heinemann, London.

Sconce J., 2000: *Haunted media. Electronic presence from telegraphy to television*, Duke University Press, Durham.

Sepstrup P., 1990: *Transnationalization of Television in Western Europe*, John Libbey, London.

Silverstone R., Hirsch E. (eds.), 1992: *Consuming technologies*, Routledge, London.

Silverstone, R. , 1994: *Television and everyday life,* Routledge, London.

Sinclair J., Jacka E., Cunningham S., 1996: *Global television. Peripheral vision*, Oxford University Press, Oxford.

Smith A., 1995: *The native are restless*, 'Media Studies Journal', fall, pp. 1–5.

Smith A. (ed.), 1995: *Television. An international history*, Oxford University Press, Oxford.

Sorice M., 2002: *Lo specchio magico. Linguaggi, formati, generi, pubblici della televisione italiana*, Editori Riuniti, Rome.

Spigel L., 1992: *Make room for tv*, The University of Chicago Press, Chicago.

Sreberny A., 2002: *Media imperialism*, in Miller T. (ed.): *Television studies*, BFI, London, pp. 21–24.

Srinivas, L., 2002: *The Active Audience: Spectatorship, Social Relations and the Experience of Cinema in India*, in 'Media, Culture and Society', 24, 2, pp 155–173.

Stevenson N., 1995: *Understanding media cultures. Social theory and mass communications*, Sage, London.

Straubhaar J., 1991: *Beyond Media Imperialism: Asymmetrical Interdependence and Cultural Proximity*, 'Critical Studies in Mass Communication', 8 (1), pp. 39–59.

Straubhaar J., 1992: *Asymmetrical interdependence and cultural proximity: a critical review of the international flow of TV programs*, paper presented at the conference of the Asociación Latinoamericana de Investigatores de la Comunicación, São Paolo.

Straubhaar J., 1996: *Distinguishing the Global, Regional and National Levels of World Television*, paper presented at the conference of the ICA, Chicago.

Straubhaar, J., 1998: *Cultural capital, language and cultural proximity in the globalization of television*, paper presented at the ICA Conference, Jerusalem.

Sturken M., Thomas, D., Ball-Rokeach, S. J. (ed.), 2004: *Technological Visions*, Temple University Press, Philadelphia.

Thompson J. B., 1995: *The Media and Modernity*, Polity Press, London.

Tichi C., 1991: *Electronic hearth. Creating an american television culture*, Oxford University Press, Oxford.

Tomlinson J., 1991: *Cultural imperialism: a critical introduction*, Pinter, London.

Tomlinson, J., 1994: *A phenomenology of globalization. Giddens and global modernity*, 'European Journal of Communication', vol. 9, pp. 149–172.

Tomlinson, J., 1999: *Globalization and culture*, Polity Press, Cambridge.

Tracey, M., Redal, W., 1995: *The new parochialism: the triumph of the populist in the flow of international television*, 'Canadian Journal of Communicatio'", vol. 20, n. 3.

Tulloch J., 2000: *Watching television audiences*, Arnold, London.

Tunstall, J. (1997): *The Media are American*, Constable, London.

Turnaturi G.., 2003: *Immaginazione sociologica e immaginazione letteraria*, Laterza, Bari.

Turner, V. (2001): *Il processo rituale*, Marcelliana, Brescia.

Turow J., 1997: *Breaking up America*, The University of Chicago Press, Chicago.

Urry J., 2000: *Sociology beyond societies*, Routledge, London.

Urry, J., 1995: *Consuming places*, Routledge, London.

Van Dijk J., de Vos L., 2001: *Searching for the Holy Grail: images of interactive television*, "New media and society", n. 4 (4), December, pp. 443–465.

Varis T., 1986: *International flow of television programmes*, reports and papers on mass communication n. 100, Unesco, Paris.

Veyne, P., 1984: *Did the Greeks believe in their myths?* Translated from French by Paula Wissing, University of Chicago Press, Chicago, 1988.

Wolton D., 1990: *Eloge du grand public*, Flammarion, Paris.

Vovelle M., 1993: *La morte e l'occidente*, Bari, Laterza.

Wang G.., Servaes J., Goonasekera A. (eds.), 2002: *The new communication landscape*, Routledge, London.

Wang G.., Yeh E., 2005: *Globalization and hybridization in cultural products*, 'International Journal of Cultural Studies', vol. 8, n. 2, pp. 175–193.

Webster J. G., 2005: *Beneath the veneer of fragmentation: television audience polarization in a multichannel world*, 'Journal of Communication', n. 2 (55), June, pp. 366–382.

White H., 1987: *The content of the form*, Johns Hopkins University Press, Baltimore.

White M., 2001: *Flows and other close encounters with television*, http://cms.mit.edu/conf/mit2/Abstracts/MimiWhite.pdf.

Williams R., 1974: *Television. Technology and cultural form*, Fontana, London; later editions Routledge, London, 1990; Wesleyan University Press, Hanover, 1992.

Williams R., 1983: *Towards 2000*, Hogarth Press, London.

Wolf M. , 1992: *Gli effetti sociali dei media*, Bompiani, Milano.

Yoshimi S., 2003: *Television and nationalism. Historical change in the national domestic tv formation of post-war Japan*, "European Journal of Cultural Studies", vol. 6, n. 4, pp. 459–487.

Zerubavel E., 1985: *Hidden Rhythms: Schedules and calendars in social life*, University of California Press, Berkeley, California.

Names Index